Hc

Stories of Healing from Eating Dis...

Co-edited by Catherine Brown and Christina Tinker

ISBN: 978-0-578-53351-3

Front cover image by Rachel Bondi.

Printed by IngramSpark, in the United States of America.

First printing edition, 2019.
hoperecoverybook.com

Table of Contents

Hope for Recovery

She Feeds on Ashes
Krista Hutcherson

If You Could See Me
Christina Tinker

Dedications

Catherine:

For years I have dreamed of putting together a book of essays by people who have been affected by eating disorders. Because the topic has come up in so many casual and in-depth conversations I have had in the past couple of decades, I knew a project like this could impact many lives.

It was serendipitous when I first met Christina Tinker in 2016 and realized we shared that dream. It took time for both of us to make the dream a priority, but we finally did. We are grateful to have gathered these wonderfully written essays by brave women and men who have shared their darkest thoughts and experiences to help those suffering. We hope their essays will not only bring hope to sufferers but also strength and insights to their loved ones.

I dedicate this book to my parents and sister, who have always supported me; my husband, who has carried the weight of recovery with me for many decades; my friends, who lift me up with their authenticity and willingness to listen and share their struggles; all those affected by eating disorders; and, my three engaging and strong-willed daughters: may you always stay strong and true to yourselves as you navigate the joys and challenges of life.

Christina:

The first time I told a friend about my battle with anorexia and bulimia, I remember thinking she would be repulsed by my story and likely choose to walk away from our friendship. I was 19 years old, and I had known this friend since elementary school. When she didn't turn away but instead offered love and grace, I thought I might die from the shame of telling her my dirty secret. I guess a part of me wanted her to push me away. She was basically my last real friend. I had battled anorexia since age 15, and the disease had stolen every friend I ever had, as it required total and complete isolation to continue slowly killing my soul and making my body smaller and smaller.

It would be more than 10 years before I told another friend about my past. At the age of 30, I had been living in full recovery for more than three years, and I had just become a mother. A small group of women had welcomed me into their circle, and one night over carrot sticks and hummus, I shared my story with the friend I had grown most close to in that circle. Again, a beautiful friend I feared might think me disgusting and weak opened her heart and embraced me with her grace.

Then, something I never expected happened. As tears streamed down her cheeks, she shared that she'd also struggled with body image in college and abused her body by starvation and excessive exercise. She said that night was the first time she'd ever told another soul about her battle. It was in that moment that I knew sharing my story could bring hope and help to others facing similar battles.

When I met Catherine Brown, I had been publicly sharing my story for several years as a speaker and writer. I had even created a non-profit organization that allowed me to speak to hundreds of teenage boys and girls throughout central Texas on the topic of eating disorder awareness.

Sharing my story with Catherine was another moment of connection I didn't see coming. As we've worked on this project together, I've grown so much in my compassion for the stories of other women and men whose stories are similar—but not the same—as mine. I received healing and hope through the sharing of the stories we've been so honored to collect and now share with you.

I dedicate this book to every friend who ever heard my story and chose to love me anyway. I dedicate this book to my mother and father who refused to give up on me and helped me find recovery, and to my younger brother and sister who suffered the grief of a sister in pain and took away some of the time and attention they wanted and needed. And lastly, I dedicate this book to my husband and three children—your unconditional love and constant encouragement of my ruthless desire to cultivate courage in our family give me hope for a bright and beautiful future.

Acknowledgements

A special thank you to Deanna Linville, Ph.D., LMFT, Associate Professor of Marriage and Family Therapy at the University of Oregon and eating disorder specialist, and Suzanne Mazzeo, Ph.D, Professor and Director of the Counseling Psychology Program at Virginia Commonwealth University and Editor-in-Chief of *Eating Behaviors*, for reviewing the essays and sharing their expertise.

In putting together this book, we set out to gather honest and intimate portrayals of eating disorders and recovery for two reasons: 1) to help those suffering understand they are not alone and can successfully recover and 2) to help friends and family understand what their loved one with an eating disorder might be experiencing.

Whenever a person writes about eating disorders, there is potential for the content to be interpreted in different ways than it was intended and for it to be in some way triggering. When developing this book, we have worked with two licensed mental health professionals with specialties in eating disorders. They have provided feedback and helped us eliminate potentially triggering material, such as specific details regarding weight, calories, specific disordered behaviors, and amounts of food consumed. It is possible, however, that some of the content in this book will be triggering to readers.

The views and descriptions expressed in the essays are those of the individual authors alone. In each essay, the writers have shared their unique experiences and the strategies of recovery that have worked best for them. Please note that some of the content involves traumatic experiences and may not be appropriate for some readers.

While these stories are written with the intent of helping readers find hope for recovery, they are not meant to replace expert advice from mental health and medical professionals. They are highly personal accounts of how these specific individuals found healing. We encourage all who are suffering from eating disorders to receive the expert help they need to recover.

I finally have reached a point where most of the time I feel fine—and even good—about who I am. I finally feel like I'm enough.

—Catherine Brown

Good Enough

Catherine Brown

Even though I have envisioned this kind of project for years, I procrastinated before sitting down to write my own essay. Like many of us, I need more hours in the day to manage my career, raise my kids, and take care of my house.

But it wasn't merely lack of time that held me back. I didn't know if I could share my experience and thoughts in a way these writers have. Their essays are honest and deep and vulnerable.

So, here goes. It's not easy to dig down and go back to a place of so much pain, but it's important. Sharing these experiences reminds all of us we're not alone. Shedding light on our darkness helps us all make our way to the other side.

There wasn't much darkness for me during the early years. I went through much of my childhood blissfully unaware of calories or fat grams. I was always naturally slim and active, so I never thought too much about my body.

Until adolescence. Like most teenage girls, I did spend an inordinate amount of time worrying about whether I was pretty enough. Or cool enough. Or likeable enough. I was painfully shy and suffered from social anxiety, though at the time I didn't even know that was a thing. I think I would have struggled more in high school had I not had a handful of close friends and strong connections with people I had known my whole life. I've always preferred deep conversations with a few close friends to small talk with lots of people, and I had enough strong connections to keep me relatively sane.

When I left my small, comfortable life to attend college, worries about my inadequacies grew substantially. I went to the best school I could get into, and that meant I was surrounded by people who were at my level or above academically and otherwise. I did have some friends who went to the same school, but I left behind several of my closest, most connected friends. I also left a loving family with pretty tight rules for a complete free-for-all.

I didn't handle it well.

The first year and a half of college, I partied pretty hard. For the first time ever, this shy, socially anxious girl had found a way to feel comfortable and confident in big groups: alcohol. It was like a new and improved me could appear on the scene every weekend and make up for all the socially awkward moments I experienced while sober.

It was fun.

For a while.

Then, it got old. I tend to be an all-or-nothing kind of gal, so I couldn't drink one or two beers and call it a night. Because of my excessive drinking, I wasn't healthy any more. I would waste a day or more recovering from parties, so my academic work suffered. And the interactions I had while drinking weren't usually that meaningful.

After engaging in the party scene for longer than I should have, I decided I would punish myself for a night of drinking by going running the next morning. It was miserable. Over time, though, I drank less at night so I could run more easily and farther the next day. Eventually, I no longer wanted to drink at all.

Exercise helped me develop some structure, but the social anxiety and insecurities that led to my overindulgence in alcohol remained. It took only a few months for an exercise addiction to set in and for a realization to happen...If I couldn't be pretty enough, smart enough, talented enough, outgoing enough, cool enough, I could be thin enough. That felt like something I could control.

So I exercised a lot and ate as little as possible to survive. I no longer went to parties, or if I did, I was home early because I was so exhausted from exercising so much and eating so little.

There were two things at play: 1) I felt like being as thin as possible would make up for all that I lacked and 2) I kinda wanted to disappear. I had made a few meaningful connections at school—I really lucked out with my roommate my first year— but in that year and a half of partying, I had slipped further away from myself and felt out of place everywhere.

It probably didn't help that I lived at my sorority house during this time. I was part of a great group of women, and I don't blame them for my eating disorder. It isn't easy, though, to be surrounded by other college-age women and not have some food or body issues. I was still so socially anxious that mealtimes felt overwhelmingly difficult. *Who would I talk to during dinner? Would I have anything to say? Who would want me to sit with them when I had so little to contribute to conversation?* It was easier to avoid meals altogether.

Because I no longer enjoyed partying and avoided group mealtimes, I became less and less connected. Looking back, I can see that loneliness and isolation played a huge role in the development of my eating disorder. The more isolated I became and the more consumed I became with trying to control my eating and exercise, the stronger the eating disorder grew.

I was so withdrawn that the people surrounding me felt uncomfortable talking to me about what I was going through. I have since had multiple people tell me they wanted to help during that time but didn't know how. I don't know exactly what went through their minds, but I imagine they had trouble confronting me because I was so withdrawn and closed off from the outside world.

And sometimes people's attempts to help were unsuccessful. At one point, some of my friends had called another close friend from high school and encouraged him to visit me. I hadn't spoken to this friend in about a year or so, but, before I went to college, we had had a strong friendship. He was the kind of person I could talk to about anything, and he knew me better than most.

I was nervous when he called to say he was visiting; I was afraid of how the interaction would go, but part of me was hopeful. Hopeful he would be the person who was comfortable enough to say, "Hey—are you okay? What's going on with this whole eating thing?"

From what I remember, the interaction was short. We chatted for a few minutes. I was admittedly cold and withdrawn, and I think he was truly at a loss for words. He left without any deep conversation having taken place, and my heart sank. The loneliness intensified. If he couldn't find a way to talk to me about this, was I even worth saving?

I realize now I put an immense amount of pressure on this friend. We hadn't talked in a while, and, as I have since learned, he felt shock from seeing me. He later told me it didn't seem like the person he knew was there at all. Now I see the courage it took for him to even come talk to me, but, at the time, it affirmed a message I was repeatedly telling myself...I would always be alone and isolated from the rest of the world.

This friend wasn't the only person to try to help. My close friends from high school did reach out, and I visited with them during that difficult period. While their connection and love helped me survive, because of their physical distance, they couldn't help me through the day-to-day experience.

My sorority sisters also tried to help by bringing in a speaker for one of our meetings. While I appreciate the effort they put forth and the stress they must have experienced trying to figure out how to help, that meeting was painful.

During the presentation, we had to split up into groups for small-group discussions. Here we were listening to a woman talking about eating disorders. They knew I had an eating disorder. I knew they had brought in this woman in part because of my eating disorder (I was not the only person suffering, but, because I had lost so much weight for my body frame, I was the most obvious sufferer at that time).

When the speaker told us to get into groups, I looked to the people around me, as you do whenever it's time to form groups. When I did, I could see the discomfort on their faces. It was so clear they didn't want to be in my group. Having this discussion about eating disorders with someone suffering from an eating disorder and not wanting to talk to that person about their eating disorder was obviously awkward for them. I don't blame them. I would have struggled in the same situation. But it was incredibly painful and isolating.

I understand how hard it is to approach someone who is suffering, but really all I needed was for a friend to ask how I was and maybe push a little for a real answer. I know I was not easy to confront or talk to at that time, but that truly is when I needed it most.

By the grace of God, I was able to talk about my struggles with my mother one day. Though many years have passed, I vividly remember standing in my room alone—my two roommates at the time were at class. I was holding the phone and looking at myself in the mirror, and I said to her, "Mom, I think I have a problem, and I need to get better." I don't even know why I said that so openly. I think I had a moment of clarity when I realized I didn't want to keep disappearing from the world both physically and psychologically.

It turns out I called at the exact moment my mom had finished a novena that I would recover.

My mom did everything right in that conversation. She listened and talked without judgement. Although I don't really remember what we talked about, I do remember just feeling better than I had for a long time. I finally felt connected to someone else again.

Shortly thereafter, I traveled with my parents to visit my newborn niece. My dad drove me, and on the way, we stopped at a diner. My dad has always been a great source of support, but he had never talked much about his emotions. While we were sitting there, he talked to me about times when he hadn't felt good enough and pursued outward accomplishments to feel better about himself. That was such a revelation to me. He is an intelligent, successful, generous person, and it seemed shocking that he would struggle with not feeling like he was enough.

The combination of those conversations and seeing my baby niece rocked me. I had always known I wanted kids, and I was devastated by the thought that I may have destroyed my chances of ever having a baby because of what I had done to my body. And now, in the amazing way the universe works, the baby girl whose birth helped me emerge from a period of intense darkness and self-loathing has created the illustration for this book's front cover.

With the support of my family and a few close friends, I started to slowly turn the ship around and follow a different course. A few months later, I met the man who became my husband, and that relationship made a huge impact. He loves cooking, and he was able to help me regain some normalcy around food. The joy of connecting so closely with him also helped me become healthier.

From the outside, it seemed like I was fixed, just like that. Lickety-split. Without any therapy or anything. And in some ways, that's true. I stopped starving myself. I ate more normally. I still exercised, but I ate, and I started to live life more fully.

Life moved on quickly, and before I knew it, I was engaged and then married and working. The starving myself changed...the feelings that drove me to starve myself didn't change as much as I would have liked. Young adulthood is difficult, and being married is wonderful and exciting but also challenging.

If I could change anything, I would go back and work with a therapist to overcome my insecurities. I would work on feeling strong and good enough without the outward accomplishments because for many years after finishing college, I teetered on the brink of being emotionally healthy and barely managed my recovery.

Fortunately, I was able to consistently stay in a healthy place, and every new experience made me a little stronger. Moving to a different part of the country, for instance, helped me figure out how to make new friends and forge strong connections with people I hadn't known for most of my life.

I had kids, and a strength I never knew I had intensified and grew. I am absolutely committed to raising my girls with a healthy body image, so I avoid talking about feeling fat or having eaten too much or any of those traps women so often fall into. I have learned the things you say to yourself and those close to you impact your emotions, for better or for worse.

Finding my passion in writing and reestablishing deep connections with old friends has also made me stronger. I finally have reached a point where most of the time I feel fine—and even good—about who I am. I finally feel like I'm enough.

I do still sometimes struggle, though. I will never starve myself again partly because my body can't seem to tolerate not being fed every few hours. I end up with a monster headache, which I think is my body's way of revolting after being mistreated.

I do sometimes obsess about losing a few pounds, and sometimes when I have trouble managing difficult emotions, I end up eating mindlessly instead of coping with my feelings.

Now, however, I can acknowledge the difficult emotions and unhealthy coping mechanisms. I forgive myself when I mess up, and I readjust by reminding myself that one bad choice does not have to lead to others. I also find it helpful to be open with myself and others about my feelings and experiences.

I manage difficult emotions and challenging tendencies by focusing each day on self-care. I have figured out what I need to thrive: physical activity; good, healthy food; quality time with family; and connections with good friends. Every day, I make those things a priority.

Recovery is a long, arduous process that involves forgiveness and love—of yourself and others in your life. I wish you all peace as you embark on your journey, and I hope these essays will help you find hope for recovery.

Catherine Brown raises three kids and writes about the arts, parenting, health and wellness, and fascinating people. She's a regular on the Zumba scene and an occasional tap dancer. Her next book project will be a compilation of essays about body image.

Compassion: An Ingredient to Eating Disorder Recovery

Elisha Contner Wilkins, MS, LMFT, CEDS-S

Recovery from an eating disorder requires ongoing support, validation, grace, and compassion. Just like many other disorders, eating disorders are often fueled by the belief that one is not worthy of love, kindness, and compassion. The eating disorder recovery process is often fraught with misunderstanding and myths that fuel an invalidating environment, leading those suffering to believe they cannot recover or are not worthy of recovery. Recovery is a journey, not a straight and narrow path, but a difficult journey that can ultimately lead to a life worth living. It is not always an uphill battle but a journey filled with missteps, wrong turns, and roadblocks. It is the hope of the destination that empowers people in recovery each and every day. And, full recovery is possible!

Compassion is a necessary ingredient of treatment and recovery. It is the foundation of the therapeutic relationship. The compassion, kindness, and validation espoused in the therapeutic relationship breeds self-compassion in those with whom we work. By demonstrating compassion towards our patients, we can teach those who have not had role models for compassion and empathy to learn self-compassion. The compassion one receives from others is transformed into self-compassion, which is an important ingredient for this journey. Self-compassion teaches us we are worthy of recovery and worthy of a life worth living and extends beyond the self to friends, family, and the greater society.

I am honored to have been a part of the recovery journey for many people over the years, and I am humbled to share this message of hope. I am grateful for those who have been open and willing to share their stories of recovery with me and the world. It is through inspirational stories that those who continue to fight this battle find solace, self-worth, validation, support, understanding, and a sense of hope.

Elisha Contner Wilkins, MS, LMFT, CEDS-S, is a Licensed Marriage and Family Therapist and Certified Eating Disorder Specialist-Supervisor. She has almost 20 years of experience working with children, adolescents, adults, and families. She serves as Executive Director, Veritas Collaborative-Virginia.

I've recognized, as a mother, that I can nurture myself like I have my three sons. I can welcome my flaws, my beauty. I can also be my own ally, my own support, because I know without a doubt that I will be with me, all of me, including that old woman in the mirror, the remaining days of my life.

—Rebecca Evans

Unempty

Rebecca Evans

This is the first week I haven't thrown up, a habit of mine spanning two decades. I'm pregnant. I'm trying to stay busy, distracted. *Do something physical; get out of the kitchen, leave the house, keep moving.* I've discovered that running and weight-lifting are "allowed" during pregnancy, so long as you maintain your previous activity level.

I will run.

Despite my lifelong draw to fitness, I've managed self-destruction through food. Some say an eating disorder demonstrates a need for control. Mine was more. I needed to unfeel my childhood pain and manage my emotions. Once in the Air Force, the stress and pressure of work and compliance tipped me. Food restriction and purging became my drugs of choice, my way to regulate. I could starve, control what I took in, and, more importantly, control what I pulled back out.

*****

Twenty years earlier, while in the military, I remember holding up my jeans, the legs dangling against my body, and stepping into them, noticing the size on the silky tag. I pulled them over my bony hips. I slipped into them without unfastening. Almost there. I smiled.

One side of my closet door framed a full-length mirror. I took two hesitant steps and filled the glass. Hand on hip, I pushed my chest out, lifting my chin, casting shadows across my collarbone. I looked vogue. I turned, glanced over my shoulder, tucked my hands in my rear pockets, and arched my back to create a deeper angle between hips and waist. I could finally see light peek between my thighs. I nodded.

Drawn to mirrors, I rarely resisted a glimpse—even when I dreaded what I might see. I sought my reflection everywhere, in shop display cases, even in the windows of parked cars, any place to pause and detect trouble spots on my body. Tiny sacks of dimpled fat seemed continuously apparent, regardless of how little I weighed. Not on this day, though. On this day, I felt small enough.

*****

I'm not sure if my struggle stemmed from the size of me or the size of my emotions. Maybe it was an attempt to retain a vacant feeling.

To be Emotionless.

If I felt happy, I'd celebrate and eat.

Sad? I turned to food.

Angry? I'd feast.

Depressed? I'd seek dessert buffets.

Proud of myself? Sometimes, these moments incited my worst binges. I felt unworthy and undeserving of accomplishment. Stuffing food into me helped snuff out any encouragement I accidently offered myself.

I lived with this sense of duplicity. In the Air Force, I was known as a fast-burner (an overachiever). I'd been awarded Below-the-Zone (early promotion), the Inspector General's Award for Excellence, Flight Data Coordinator of the Year, etc. I held accolades, "trophies" to prove my worth. I was great at pretending everything was "fine," yet I lived with fear that the military would realize my falseness and discharge me. To me, the military had become my mother, my father, my family. I became meticulous at hiding my malady.

*****

One day, I shopped at the BX, the Base Exchange, the Air Force's version of an American department store, a luxury while stationed in the UK. I walked to the Exchange, as I hadn't enough money left over from groceries to afford car payments. Besides, walking kept me shapely, tightening the stringy muscles in my legs.

With a basket in the crook of my arm, I selected a few bright scarves and belts. I took my time, knowing when the spree ended I would be alone and the fight with bingeing and purging would ensue. Again. As I walked towards the stack of Calvin Kleins, I passed an old woman, or it could have been an old man, limbs like twigs, so thin I thought they would surely break.

I stopped, stared at the woman, and the woman stopped and stared back.

Then I understood: this aged and hollowed human was my reflection. I quickly raised my hand, covered my mouth, and a weak, barely audible cry escaped. In my home, I could conjure some beautiful and healthy woman I inevitably saw, as if seeing myself from a great distance. Here, in public, encountering my image without warning, I was shocked by my darkly malnourished frame. The grave image before me was proof. I finally saw an accurate picture of my physical self. A surge of fear pulsed through me.

I look like hell.

How did I not see myself this way?

I set the basket at my feet, my mirror-me repeating the gesture. I negotiated the clothing racks and display mannequins, navigating towards the exit, trembling. I walked tenderly, suddenly fragile, as if something inside me might crack.

I strode across the street to the hospital, stood in the entrance, tugging my shirt to cover my exposed mid-section. I told the receptionist I needed to see someone today, as I hadn't had time to schedule an appointment.

"What kind of symptoms are you having?"

"Just flu-like symptoms," I said. "I'm having a hard time keeping food down. I'm okay."

The "receptionist," a young female sergeant in hospital whites, regarded me for the first time, stretching her neck to see over the counter. She started to write something on the log in front of her, apparently changed her mind, and with what looked like a concerned expression, examined me again. She tapped the pencil against her bottom lip.

"I know the perfect doctor for you," she said. "Let me see if she can squeeze you in."

*****

The nurse took my temperature, height, and then weight. When I stepped onto the scale, I shut my eyes. Minutes later, Dr. B walked through the door, her white coat unbuttoned, floating open on each side. She carried a petite frame with a narrow waist, flat chest, and full hips. I was born thick-waisted, athletic in form. I spent a lifetime chiseling out a curve.

"You're not eating?" Dr. B asked, flipping the single page in my medical chart.

"I haven't felt well in a while."

"How long is a while?" She drew her stethoscope to her ears and stood, placing the instrument over my heart.

I shrugged. *Maybe coming to the hospital was a mistake.*

"You're clicking. Have you always had a murmur?"

"I don't think so."

When she gently tapped under my eye, it felt as though a streak of lightning seared through my head. I tried not to flinch. She leaned back. A burst of small sparkles formed, and I blinked them away, bringing the room back to focus. Air Force blue walls, one stool, one examination table (where I sat), a stainless-steel sink, wall-mounted sterilizing hand soap, and a counter lined with glass jars filled with cotton balls, throat swabs, and tongue depressors.

"How badly did that hurt?" she asked.

"It didn't."

"Your eyes look swollen underneath. Do you suffer with allergies, maybe some sinus pressure?"

"I could."

She pulled each lid back, peered inside, as if looking for a different answer.

"When was the last time you ate a meal?" she asked.

"I don't usually eat meals. I'm kind of a grazer, you know. I snack all day."

"Do you ever feel hungry?"

"No."

"All right then. Here's the deal. Your weight is critically low. You have heart palpitations. I'd like to get some blood work, okay?"

I exhaled.

"Something's going on with you. Do you want to talk about it?" she asked.

"I'm good," I responded.

"Are you sure?" she asked.

When I didn't answer, she began to write in her chart.

I knew she could never understand that I only did what I did as an attempt to look my best. After all, it wasn't as if overeating could compare to over-drinking. With alcohol, you just stopped. Food needed to be spooned in throughout the day, controlled, disciplined in portions and choices. I navigated my "condition" with far greater mental acuity than your average addict.

She didn't ask if I'd been throwing up. She didn't ask if I was starving myself, and, if I was, why. My shoulders relaxed. I didn't need too much help anyway. I wanted mostly to look normal.

"What are you writing in my chart? Are you writing about my weight or something?" I asked.

"I'm writing what I just told you," she said. "Are you sleeping?"

"I'm one of those people who doesn't need much sleep, just a few hours. And that works for me. I can get a lot more done on my personal time."

She quit writing, set the pen on the chart, listened. I kept talking.

"I generally like staying awake while the rest of the world sleeps," I said. "It feels like I have a great secret for my achievements...you know, like I've created more time. Sort of a superpower."

I left the hospital with a prescription for an antidepressant in hand, and, as I shuffled back to my dorm, I glanced over my shoulder several times, watching the hospital grow smaller, the sky heavy with steel-gray clouds, usual for England. Certain the doctor or receptionist would run after me any second, admit me for malnourishment or insanity, I stretched my legs long, trying to cover more ground without running, avoiding attention. Once in my room, I shut my door and waited for a sense of relief.

It never came.

Over the next two weeks, I worried even more, thinking the doctor would phone my Commanding Officer.

She did make a call, but only to me.

"With your potassium seriously low, it's a miracle your heart still gives the electrical impulses needed to simply blink. That explains the murmur," she said. "I'm adding a time-released supplement to your diet, potassium chloride." I was deficient in most every nutrient, so she prescribed prenatal vitamins as well.

It took another week before I swallowed down my dose of antidepressant. That first night, I slept for four hours in a row and felt groggy when I woke. In the morning, I wondered why I had never seen this woman in my mirror before, the old woman, ravaged in her body and her mind. My stomach growled, an unusual and uncomfortable feeling. I was uncertain if the pain in my belly signaled hunger or nausea, but I was sure this would be the day I would keep food inside. Most nights I told myself, *tomorrow will be different.* This time I knew it could. Maybe I could stay unempty. Remain in that place of health and satiation where I no longer gorged, no longer suffered my void in life.

*****

Repair did not happen on that day or that month. My mending felt more like micro-movements, degrees on a compass, as if turning myself slowly around. I had to learn how to feel emotions. All of them. Good, bad, scary. I sought treatment while in the service, then continued therapy once honorably discharged after eight years. I wanted to get well. I wanted more than anything to have acceptable eating habits.

There came a point when I binged and purged or starved only once a month, or less, and this seemed as steady as I would become. I maintained this holding pattern for almost two decades following my military career.

Until I found myself pregnant.

It was the first time I had anything else, anybody else, to care about. Unsure I was equipped to be a mother after all my years of starvation, I feared I might not have the nutrients to build a baby inside of me. I worried about feeling fat, ugly, and unlovable during my pregnancy. I feared after-delivery baby weight. I made a pact with myself that once my son was born, I could devour all the food I wanted. Surely he would nap, offering me moments to binge. I could stop once thin enough. I could stop anytime I wanted.

These are the promises I made.

Like many vows over the last two decades, I would break most.

I promise tomorrow I will be normal with food.

This one.

Almost my mantra.

*****

My son arrived, disabled, small for size, medically fragile, partially missing a gene. There was no longer room in my life for self-destruction or melancholy moments, as he could die on my watch if I didn't get my act together.

The truth is, I couldn't. Those early years of his life, I frantically tried to keep him alive while keeping it "all together." Through his (now) thirty-six surgeries, there simply wasn't time or space to disintegrate.

I've had setbacks: kidney surgery, hip surgery, a full hysterectomy, cervical spine surgery (twice), shoulders and knees and...

Fitness as I once knew it would no longer help me handle stress.

These days, my "routine" consists of breath-work and gentle stretching. I wrestle with accepting my body. With rest. I'm cultivating these things, still, even in my fifties.

My firstborn is now seventeen, and I've birthed two more sons. I've discovered how pain, physical or emotional, travels its course. Sometimes, though, in the midst of it, i believe I won't survive.

*****

Today, I allow emotions to run all the way through. I write out feelings instead of swallowing them down. I sort out my life on the page. This helps. Instead of emptying out, I try to fill up. I walk through my yard in the mornings, my soles brushing wet grass as I soak in flowers and tomatoes and herbs. I color with crayons, make homemade soap, create memories. The kitchen holds few moments unrelated to binges. Blank spaces. Addiction does that. My brain seemed adhered to food-focus, and I forgot to enjoy the life I was living. Luckily, in the military and since, I journaled, noted small details of people and places. Lately, I've opened those pages, perusing through my past, understanding what might have happened.

Understanding me.

The me-then.

The me-now.

When I succumb to binge-purge tendencies, I try to forgive myself. I'm learning this too. I slow down small tasks, such as washing my face, taking a few moments instead of rushing through, instead of treating my body like an inconvenience. Or allowing myself sleep, though I'm still learning to sleep. I have altered my perception of rest as a luxury. Over time, with healing, with acceptance, the compulsion to purge has become infrequent. I'm often surprised when an entire year passes and I haven't induced vomiting. I'm even more astonished after a month free from fighting mental impulses.

This is most likely the truth of all addictions. They linger. They hang around in the background like a prior, toxic friend, someone you know not to engage with, but maybe you nod, not because of a longing, but simple familiarity. I've felt it far better to face that former acquaintance and acknowledge her existence, instead of avoiding her. I've recognized, as a mother, that I can nurture myself like I have my three sons. I can welcome my flaws, my beauty. I can also be my own ally, my own support, because I know without a doubt that I will be with me, all of me, including that old woman in the mirror, the remaining days of my life.

Rebecca Evans is a decorated Air Force Veteran who mentors high school girls in the juvie system through writing. She is the recipient of the 2018 Cunningham short fiction story award. Her work can be found in The Rumpus, Entropy, The Normal School, Fiction Southeast, Tiferet Journal, Gravel, *and more. She serves on the editorial staff of the* Sierra Nevada Review *and lives in Idaho with her three sons.*

Nobody will enjoy your life for you...that's something you've got to do for yourself.

—Jacqueline Richards

A Light at the End of a Tunnel

Jacqueline Richards

I once had a friend tell me they thank God for their nervous breakdown because they became more human, more understanding, more well-rounded as a result. I never understood that until now—twenty years after my own. I am still being treated for post-traumatic stress disorder to this day, and I guess it will never go away.

Eating disorders don't really go away either. You just learn to adapt. Survive. Develop coping mechanisms.

The seed for me was bullying at school. I was always the frumpy friend. "Thunder thighs," they called me. I was the one in nightclubs they bought a drink for just to be polite, though the guys never seemed to be looking back. And this prejudice has continued to this day.

Gradually I became obsessed. I *felt* I was unattractive (not now, I'm glad to say), and vomiting was like a cleansing or purification to relieve my hurt, my bruises. I was so emotionally unstable that I released my stress like an explosion. I was frustrated. Bulimia was the ultimate tool in my defense armory. I *felt* puking was the only way I had control, and it has taken me until my middle age to realize there are better ways of being independent and maintaining self esteem.

Since my teenage years, when I suffered from bulimia, I have always been aware of mental health issues. But the causes of my acute crises during young adulthood were manifold: thefts, a burglary, obscene calls, and sexual harassment/bullying at work. All these events occurred within eighteen months of each other and precipitated my own psychiatric episode.

This was a scary period of my life. I was young and far away from home. My self-esteem was so low that it took every last bit of energy I had to live on and lift myself off the floor. So unstable was my mood that I fluctuated from elation to floods of tears and often still do; it's part of my character.

Life affects us all in different ways. How we deal with our own crises is the mark of our identity, a private matter. Everyone has their own uniqueness—ideals and values, of course—but what binds us together is our common humanity. Lots of people feel they can't cope at some time in their lives. The stigma associated with mental health has been one of the hardest things to deal with, professionally and personally, even amongst so-called caring professionals.

But I am here to tell you: it is possible to move on.

When I think back on my road to recovery there were two key events. The first was Christmas dinner. I got a grip then knowing how hard the family had tried to make the day a success. No one said anything, but I'm sure they knew I had left the table to purge. *God, forgive me for what I put my family through at this time.*

The second was when my nephew, who, at age 3, remarked "Aunty been sick." I didn't know he'd spotted me or that he possessed such vocabulary. It was the ultimate humiliation.

Small steps have brought me to a better place. Day by day. Despite the setbacks (I've probably relapsed ten times without anyone knowing), a healthy self discipline and positive mental attitude have helped.

"Nobody will enjoy your life for you...that's something you've got to do for yourself—with others not for them." This has become my mantra. Positivity. Life, love, laughter. Lots more to live for.

Max Ehrmann said, "Beyond a wholesome discipline, be gentle with yourself. You are a child of the universe. No less than the stars and the trees. You have a right to be here. And whether or not it is clear to you, no doubt it is unfolding as it should." This meditation has also been my mantra, and it still guides me.

Being in a depressed state has enabled me to put into perspective what suffering and beauty there can be in humanity. Man's basic nature is to relate to others. Ups and downs. Togetherness. The spirit of man's endurance is in his resilience.

The light at the end of my tunnel was a kind-hearted nun, my colleague and friend, who reached out her hand to me. I was truly blessed to have such an insightful and understanding companion at this time and to meet this meek, mild, and yet strong woman. She was a true matriarch in every sense of the word. Everyone needs their Sister Consilia. My friends like Sister Consilia have inspired me to see the world in a whole new light: from the depths of despair and desperation to hope, reconciliation, and acceptance. She is one of life's angels. So is my mother, though aged. Who else can see the good in you so well?

The compassion of others has helped me through my own problems. My friends, family, priests, and colleagues continue to be my Bridge Over Troubled Water. Music, along with a good diet, regular exercise, tai chi, and walking, has left me feeling better than ever. Cognitive Behavioral Therapy has helped me tackle some pretty traumatic issues. Self-discipline, regular relaxation, and a stable personal life have also helped me relate better than I ever did to others. Taking an interest in keeping fit, being honest, and staying busy are all solutions I recommend. Lots of care and lots of loving have led to a new satisfaction and happiness in my personal life.

Despite this progress, I still have glimpses and flashbacks and regularly refer to the attacks I suffered because, regardless of what has happened, I want my friends to understand who I am. Getting upset about it changes nothing. But now, more in acceptance, I am able to walk outside, go for meals, be seen in a swimsuit, drive—even at night—and yes, even work.

Just as others have their own problems, so everyone can develop their own solutions. Now I see a way forward. I myself was a victim of crime, which always destroys lives, yet there is no point in allowing this rot to destroy my inner self. Holding others accountable through peaceful, legal means takes courage...you can do it, too. Believe me. Inside, somewhere, find your inner strength. I did. I'm made of stronger stuff than jelly. I'm from rugby blood!

I hope you will also find your missing jigsaw puzzle piece, and I hope this account has helped you in doing so. Whatever or whoever guides you, and however you find your way from the doldrums to the heights, I really do hope you'll get there.

Jacqueline Richards is a UK-based writer, nurse, midwife, and children's author who has had a productive, varied, and interesting career. What is little known other than to family and close friends is that most of her life has been plagued by eating disorders; having been a victim of recurrent crime, she has been treated for anxiety, depression, and post-traumatic stress. Her message to you is that there is a light at the end of the tunnel if you can learn to love yourself and find a better way.

I look away from the reflection and remind myself that this body that confines me is strong and healthy and allows me to give and show love. It bore my sons. It allows me to give encouragement and affection through warm hugs and gentle touch.

—Misti Anderson

Living with Her

Misti Ault Anderson

At first, recovering from my eating disorder seemed almost insurmountable. Lost in the tangle of darkness and self-loathing, I struggled to see a way clear of it. Moving through the painful process of admitting to my family what I had been doing to myself was the first real step onto the long and winding road of recovery.

Naively, I thought—or perhaps hoped—that while it would be a challenge to get healthy, I would work hard and be rewarded with a fully healthy mind and body that I would no longer hate. I would approach recovery like school: I would work hard and succeed. Of course my tried-and-true methods would work; they always did.

But as it turns out, recovery is neither predictable nor a straight path. I was right about the hard work, although I underestimated it. I was wrong about the ease of success.

Twenty years later, when I turned 39, I ran my first marathon. I trained for over six months through ups and downs. There were hard days, tears, and injuries. And then there was pride, relief, and joy at the finish line. That was roughly how I had expected my recovery would go, when I was first coming to terms with my eating disorder. I knew it would be messy and hard, surely with setbacks, but I really thought there would be victory and a finish line. I was wrong.

Looking back, I can see the years it took for my eating disorder to develop. Like a film that plays in my memory, I watch it emerge and change over time. It wasn't fast; it grew slowly and took over like an invasive species. I can see how my parents missed it. I can understand how they didn't see it even when I dropped a significant amount of weight within the span of a year.

It is painful for me still, even now after almost three decades have passed, to think about it. Both the before and after numbers make me cringe, if for different reasons. Weight is just a number! It means nothing. It does not reflect my worth as a human being—it didn't then, and it doesn't now. Of course I know this. And these statements are true. But I'd be lying if I told you I could refer to my weight at any moment in time without the pang of anxiety.

The truth is that I was bulimarexia for years and now am a middle-aged mother with a wonderful family and a successful career—and I still use a variety of tools to actively manage the residual anxiety related to my eating disorder. That's the part they won't tell you and that many don't acknowledge. Managing recovery is a lifelong commitment. It is worth it, without a doubt. But it is relentless.

I protect myself with safeguards. For example, I don't own a scale, and I never will. I have come close to purchasing one in the past, but I came to my senses and resisted the urge. The prospect of numerical data remains dangerous for me. Owning a scale would lead to measurement and tracking. Those numbers are emotional landmines, no matter how certain I am that they do not define me or reflect my worth. I have learned to not put myself in that position.

Another self-imposed safeguard is to carefully monitor my approach to exercise. For me, exercise was once both a punishment for eating and another way to purge, so in recovery I had to break those associations. I learned to be active without being regimented. I learned to build a wall between food and exercise, to not keep a running tally of what I'd eaten and what I would need to do later to burn it off. Eventually I developed a healthy relationship with exercise: I do fun, active things I enjoy with people I love. I run to manage my stress, for "me" time, and to spend much-needed time with my dear friend and running partner. I am extremely careful not to create a regimen of exercise habits. Rather, I have turned exercise into a tool for stress management and self care.

I have learned to be vigilant about managing my stress. Experience has taught me that high stress levels awaken my dormant disorder. My setbacks have always come in times of high stress and anxiety. So now, when I start to feel the physical manifestations of stress, I know it is time to prioritize stress relief before the voices of self-doubt and self-destruction creep into my mind.

I allow myself only one exercise-related rule: forward motion is good. It need not be fast or graceful or pretty, only forward.

Forward motion is good. That rings true for me both literally and figuratively. Recovery is all about forward motion. Little steps. Each day I run to shed stress from my mind and body so that it doesn't wear down the resolve that supports my recovery is a win. Each day that I eat healthy, substantial meals with a snack or two—and maybe a sweet treat with my children—is a win. I began my recovery 27 years ago, and every day I can do that for myself is a win. Still.

Many of the wins are easy now, and there are some days when I really don't think about it. But most days "She" (my eating disorder, that is) checks in with me mentally at some point, over some small food- or exercise-related decision. She speaks up in my moments of self-doubt, when my confidence is shaken, when I'm tired and overwhelmed. Or sometimes when I catch a sideways glance at the reflection of my middle-aged mom body in a window or mirror, hers is the first voice in my head to speak up. She can be quite loud.

But I have learned to be louder. I have learned to shout back. I hold my ground. I look away from the reflection and remind myself that this body that confines me is strong and healthy and allows me to give and show love. It bore my sons. It allows me to give encouragement and affection through warm hugs and gentle touch. When the self-doubt and pressure build, I put this body to use pounding the negativity out on the running trail. Sometimes the tears fall with the sweat. I have learned to use this body that was once my enemy as a tool to fight back against Her, where she resides in my mind.

I *will not* buy a scale and allow myself to walk into the trap of daily data assault. If my clothes fit, I'm doing just fine.

I *will* treat myself to a scoop of ice cream when I take my children to Baskin Robbins because (1) I must force myself to do and eat normal things, and (2) I refuse to demonstrate for my children recurring self-restrictive behavior. I never want to face the question: "Mom, why don't you ever get a treat?"

I *will not* eat past the point of "full." I simply can't. Even after all these years, my body doesn't react well to the feeling of "too full." Too full means an hour or more of slow, deep breathing to prevent myself from vomiting. It takes concentration and effort and, more importantly, it takes me away from focusing on life and laughter with friends and family, or just enjoying the moment.

I *will* exercise regularly for fitness, stress and anxiety relief, time with my friend, and my own sanity. But I *will not* establish a regimen of daily runs with distance, time, and calorie-burning requirements. I won't.

I. Will. Not.

So many rules!

I manage my recovery though carefully set rules for myself. Decades ago, I used self-imposed rules to attack myself through my eating disorder. Now I use self-imposed rules to keep Her at bay and manage my recovery. I've made my peace with Her. She is always here with me. I've had to befriend Her, learn from Her, and acknowledge Her co-existence so I can get on with my life. Forward motion.

Over all these years, there has been only one other person with whom I could talk openly, completely, and comfortably about my eating disorder. He is a dear friend, a former colleague, and a recovering addict. For a long time, he shared his personal experiences and story with me. He was open and honest and did not hold back. It was humbling to be chosen to share and sit with the weight of his experience—to be entrusted with it.

It took years of friendship before I shared my story with him. He listened to me and, after a long pause, thanked me for sharing. He told me that over the years he sensed I wasn't a normal earthling (his term for non-addicts) but could never figure out how that could be since I wasn't an addict. He smiled warmly and kindly at me and enveloped me into one of the most meaningful hugs I have ever received. I felt understood, loved, and forgiven all at once. I had spoken one of my most painful secrets and been received with warmth and care rather than dismay. It was a powerful lesson for me.

It was that friend that encouraged me to let Her in and walk with Her for a while. He shared with me a powerful metaphor for doing this which, he said, applied to both his addiction and my eating disorder. Paraphrasing, it goes something like this: *my addiction/disorder is present and cannot be denied. If I push it out of my mind and lock it up in a dark room, it will spend its time pumping iron, growing in strength and power, until it breaks through the door and overpowers me again. But if I let it remain with me, get to know it better, I can draw upon its presence and maybe some of its characteristics as tools to anchor myself and grow and recover and get through today without harming myself.*

So I let Her out. I got to know Her. And I use Her. Unabashedly. She is ever-present in the back of my mind, sitting quite close to my imposter complex, chatting away. She is a part of me—part of my story and my journey. I remain vigilant about the power she wields and, in doing so, I continue my recovery every day, one at a time. Forward motion.

Today I will eat, I will play, I will find joy, and I will forgive myself yet again.

Misti is a happy, conflicted, and overwhelmed working mom just like all the others. She is buoyed by her faith, family, and friends, and she tries to make the world just a little bit brighter one day at a time. And when that doesn't work, she gets up and tries again.

Males and Eating Disorders

"There is an inaccurate belief that males do not suffer from eating disorders," says Andrew Walen, LCSW-C, LICSW, CEDS, Founder and Executive Director of the Body Image Therapy Center. For years, experts believed that one in ten people suffering from eating disorders is male. Walen explains that research has since found that males make up one-third of the people suffering from anorexia and bulimia, half of those suffering from bingeing disorder, and two-thirds of people who have avoidant/restrictive feeding and intake disorder (ARFID).

Body image issues that contribute to eating disorders can look different for men than for women. Men, for instance, tend to focus on leanness and muscularity. "Men aren't fixated as much on weight but rather on the 'show-me' muscles, like abs, biceps, and pectorals," says Walen. "Typically about half of men who restrict or purge want to get leaner, while the other half want to build up their muscles and get bigger."

Diagnosing eating disorders among males can be problematic. Men typically don't recognize their eating as disordered because compulsive exercise and binge eating have been normalized for males, particularly those involved in athletics. In addition, heterosexual men may be unwilling to acknowledge their struggle because they tend to see eating disorders as affecting only women and gay men. "Going into treatment for an eating disorder feels like the antithesis of masculinity," Walen says.

It doesn't help that treatment programs tend to be geared toward women. When men do seek help for eating disorders, they tend to feel uncomfortable or unwelcome. Often the physical space has been designed to appeal to women, and the conversation can be more relevant to women who suffer. "Men often feel dismissed because they don't use the same language to talk about eating disorders and their bodies," Walen says.

According to Walen, less than 1% of all research on eating disorders involves males. Walen is hopeful these statistics will change given that several prominent athletes have recently shared their stories. Mike Marjarma, a former catcher from the Seattle Mariners, for instance, made headlines when he shared his story of restricting and purging in order to achieve a perfect physique. In 2018, he retired from baseball to work full-time as an ambassador for the National Eating Disorders Association. Patrick Devenney from the Seattle Seahawks also shared his story of binge eating and body image struggles.

As Mike Marjarma has explained in his talks about eating disorders, it is not always obvious when a man is suffering from an eating disorder. When Marjarma was severely restricting his diet, his family and friends could not recognize his struggles simply by looking at him. Walen encourages concerned parents and loved ones to be aware of the signs of a possible eating disorder, which include personality and body changes, anger, and unstable moods.

If you see these signs in a loved one, talk to him openly. "It's appropriate to confront that person by saying, 'I'm concerned about you, and I love you,'" Walen says. It is best to avoid making comments about the person's weight, however, because those comments can elicit feelings of shame and discourage the sufferer from admitting there is a problem.

Walen encourages men affected by eating disorders to find a specialist who has experience working with males. "Eating disorders can be easily dismissed in males," he says, "even by professionals who are trained to look at eating disorders."

It is amazing the positivity that can form if you're willing to share.

—Francis Iacobucci

A Boy In Trouble, A Man Saved

Francis Iacobucci, MSW

Prologue

On September 30, 2015, a month before turning 30 years old, I sat at my desk and penned a letter to my wife. I said farewell to my colleagues as I did every Wednesday (albeit a little earlier than usual) and took the long walk back to my apartment building. It was a rare cool day in Washington, DC, and the tidal basin sparkled in the setting sun. I arrived home, gave our cats a good belly rub, left the letter on the counter, and headed to the roof. I leaned over the edge, observing the distance between me and the pavement below, inhaling deeply.

I braced my body, deciding on which way I wanted to fall. I took one final moment to visualize my mom, my dad, and my sisters. And through tears, I whispered goodbye.

My phone buzzed. My grip on the banister loosened. I exhaled. I answered the call. I'll never recall what was said, but that call saved my life.

There will never be enough paper or time to fully describe my eating disorder story. As with everyone's, it is complex, unique, emotional, and at times, traumatic. I do not pretend to be an expert, and I recognize how, as a white, cisgender, heterosexual male, I was generally immune to the inherent bias and marginalization often associated with mental health access and treatment. Because of this, I recognize and acknowledge the unique power in every individual's story.

This story—my story—is about a young man's struggle with acceptance and self-worth and overcoming emotional neglect; it is about the ways in which I coped with these emotional challenges; and it is about my eventual recovery and growth from binge eating disorder and bulimia nervosa. My hope is that this story will provide tangible evidence to those who struggle to recognize a future beyond this disease that recovery is possible.

The beginning

For as long as I can remember, I was fat. —journal entry, January 8, 2014

The manifestation of my eating disorder is deeply rooted in the early years of my life. I struggled with undiagnosed binge eating disorder for many years, developed as a mechanism to cope with a chaotic household. While understanding the relational dynamics of my parents, my siblings, and the foster children that came and went through our home is an ongoing topic of discussion in therapy, it is clear that food—and bingeing on it— provided an emotional outlet that cemented itself deep within me at an early age.

My parents were (and continue to be) truly amazing individuals who loved me and my sisters fiercely, and although they were concerned about my weight (they even took me to a nutritionist at age 11 or 12), eating disorders in young males were not in the minds of most parents (or most physicians) at the time, and so no clear diagnosis was made or course of treatment determined. The answer, always, was that I needed to eat healthier and exercise more. Or, as I heard it: this is your fault, so fix it yourself (interestingly, my parents likely felt it was their fault and that they needed to fix it). This sense that foods were either good or bad became a core belief, and it juxtaposed nicely with the family ritual of eating for comfort.

As I grew, I began to become overwhelmed with the size of my body, referred to as my "bigness" herein. While I certainly struggled as a young boy, a decision made in middle school changed the trajectory of my life and made early intervention nearly impossible. As a seventh grader, at nearly 200 pounds and a foot taller than every other student in my class, I was asked to join the high school wrestling team. How thrilling! I agreed, my parents agreed, the school administrators agreed, and I, a 12-year-old boy, was on the team. In a single moment I went from having no place for my bigness to exist to my bigness being sought after and lauded by adults.

My bigness had a home. My emotional development and need to cope, however, were still homeless and neglected. My binge eating remained intact as a means to stabilize my emotions—its original purpose—and was now also justified by the fact that my size was needed (in athletics, mostly). I believed my size was a reflection of who I was, and so the emotionally damaged foundation constructed years earlier continued to rage within me. My disordered eating behaviors had free reign under the guise of this need to be big—a scenario allowed by the approval of the very adults I most trusted, and on whom I depended— something that I have spent years trying to untangle in my mind. At the time, however, it was cool in a way, which led to a slow boil rather than an explosion.

The rest of middle school and then high school was a six-year stretch when I felt relatively safe from the emotional turmoil brewing inside. I was popular, had a girlfriend, and was the school's star athlete. The external experience of being big was nearly always positive. Through these attributes I gained a lot of acceptance that allowed me to suppress the emotional turmoil. Fast-forward to the end of high school, and with it the end of the protection of my bigness and the safety of my emotional deficits.

As I transitioned to college, so did my eating disorder. I learned that my size seemed to have less value when not associated with athletics, and I had spent my entire life burying my emotional wellbeing as a survival mechanism. I was crushed, and soon the need to compensate for my binge behavior became a top priority. I felt if I did not have a reason to be big, everyone was going to hate me. Purging, through vomiting, became my solution. I'm not entirely sure how I came to throwing up—which speaks to the dissociative nature of this disease. In any case, bulimia nervosa began its paralyzing grip on my physical and mental health.

The struggle

I find myself looking ahead, to a time that doesn't exist. To a life that's not real. —journal entry, August 5, 2013.

I did not become fully aware of my eating disorder for years. I had no words to describe my unhealthy eating habits, obsession about my size and appearance, and disproportionate amounts of money spent on binges (thousands and thousands of dollars over nearly a decade). Still, all of this seemed very much like a fixable problem. I associated none of it, however, with my mental health. Society tells males to never feel, or at least to never talk about our feelings. To compensate, I binged and purged and restricted and exercised obsessively three to four times daily for nearly a decade.

The subsequent years with my eating disorder were a portrait of rash decisions, manipulation, money spending, heartbreaking choices, binge drinking, and a lot of eating and throwing up. It's a lot. I think what may be most useful is to tell two stories that represent defining moments in my struggle—moments so dissociative it is hard to fathom how I was ever able to avoid facing the brutal reality that was my eating disorder.

First story.

I was 20 years old, a junior in college, broken up from my girlfriend, not excelling athletically, and essentially having a nervous breakdown numbed by my eating disorder—a disease I was not yet truly conscious about. It all felt quite overwhelming, and so I did what many individuals who cannot process emotion do: I decided to up and leave school and move to Des Moines, Iowa. In retrospect, joining then-Senator Obama's campaign for president was likely one of the better decisions I'll have ever made, though it truly is fascinating to consider that the right decision at the time would have been to stay put and seek treatment. Funny how life works!

On the eve of my first day on the job, my parents had put me up in an Embassy Suites. Naturally, I was nervous. *What if I cannot do this? Am I smart enough? God I'm so fat.* The thoughts were messy. It was the closest I felt to mania in my life. I was going mad. Then, in an instant, I looked down to see plates that held burgers, chicken fingers, French fries, Caesar salad, soup, pizza, and a dessert of some sort—all empty. The fullness—to say the least—was a needed distraction from my racing mind. *But I'm still fat.* I got up, went to the bathroom, and threw up. This, I remember, was the first time I noticed the relief. It felt good, and I wanted more. Those behaviors allowed me to get through what felt like an impossible moment and reveal how I felt most consistently with my eating disorder: totally convinced that this is how I can feel better. From that point on I sought it as a means to manage my emotions. It led to some misguided and eventually heartbreaking decisions.

Second story.

One of the decisions was marriage. Coincidently, the use of bulimia to numb myself nearly paralleled my relationship with my ex-wife. I had met her—a woman whom I consider one of the most intelligent, passionate, and important people I will ever have known—on the campaign. It took years—and a lot of manipulation on my part—for our marriage to fully deteriorate. On this particular day, two things happened. First, we realized we could not save our marriage, a gut-wrenching truth. Second, we were able to see quite clearly why our marriage was ending: I was in a relationship with my eating disorder (though it still took me months to verbalize that truth).

It began after a vicious text exchange between us, sometime in October 2015. I left work and wandered, attempting to clear my head. All I remember is my ex-wife picking me up on a street corner outside a pizza shop. I don't remember getting to the shop, or calling her, or eating (my credit card statement later indicated I had ordered two large pizzas). I do remember her pulling up and looking at me with tears in her eyes. We did not speak for the remainder of the night. In truth, we never really spoke meaningfully again. I told her thank you for picking me up. I was really saying goodbye.

There are many stories with similar details, but in that moment I recognized the connection between my emotional health and my disordered eating. It was the first time I thought maybe I have an eating disorder and maybe it's not allowing me to live freely and fully, and maybe there are other things going on I need to address.

The turning point and a farewell

I wept...it was like saying goodbye to the love of my life. — journal entry, January 31, 2016.

There I stood, atop my apartment building's roof on a brisk September evening, ready to leave it all behind—the pain, the feelings of worthlessness, the failed marriage, and the emptiness. It would all die with me. That phone call not only stopped me from jumping off the roof but allowed for a bit of much needed self-reflection, gave me the opportunity to give myself permission to seek help, and created an opening for the long path for recovery. It gave me a chance to have that moment at the pizza shop, allowing me to name this disease.

It took a while—and the end of my marriage—to fully get to a place where I felt I couldn't solve anything on my own. Finally, in early December 2015, I called a clinic that offers intensive outpatient services for individuals struggling with eating disorders and body image. On December 14, I started the treatment program. It was a big, difficult page to turn and a day I will never forget. It was the first time I had done something solely for the purpose of my well-being.

That Monday was challenging. I remember physically being at work but feeling anxious about the anticipation of intensive outpatient therapy. *What was the program like? Would I be the only male in the program (I was, on most days)? What would people think of me?* It helped that I had incredible, compassionate individuals at my place of work who recognized I was reaching out for help and granted me whatever graces I needed. Still, I was a nervous wreck.

It helped that my parents listened and were supportive—both emotionally and financially—of my decision to seek treatment. It helped that I had a few friends I felt comfortable sharing my story with (one of whom I fell in love with and can happily call my partner today). There was a lot of help from so many people—it is amazing the positivity that can form if you're willing to share. Still, it was my decision to actually attend treatment.

I went, and it was fine. We talked as a group, I learned eating disorder lingo, we ate dinner together, we reported our hunger level a few times. I went again. And again, until it was the weekend. My first weekend I binged and purged—the first and last time I did so during treatment (but not the last time I ever did). I went back the following Monday. And again, until I had completed over three months of treatment. I credit that particular therapy center for saving my life and stabilizing me. They provided techniques for how to assess eating habits, and they helped me establish safety in telling my story. Mostly, though, they indirectly allowed me to end the relationship with my eating disorder. It was time to say farewell.

I become emotional thinking about what it meant to me to say goodbye. As a young boy, faced with combating the notion that I wasn't enough, I found comfort and acceptance in eating. In middle school, faced with trying to fit in with high school men, eating a whole pizza made me feel worthy. As an adult, faced with the demons of my past, I felt cared for through a bag of burgers. All of it numbed me. Those seemingly positive emotions made the eating disorder my best friend—at times my only friend—and a friend from whom I desperately needed relief. Attempting to find new ways to cope seemed impossible with the eating disorder. It took so long to realize that living was more important than this relationship, and through writing I said goodbye, for the second time in a year.

It was the hardest, saddest thing I have ever done, and it would not have been possible without treatment and the compassion of a few individuals who gave me the space to find a way to live again. They gave me a space to find a way to recovery.

Recovery and Advocacy

It's made me think and feel – something I haven't done in a while...years, really. It's the best decision I've made. —journal entry, January 13, 2016.

At the risk of sounding obvious, I believe it is important to note that everyone experiences recovery differently. My recovery consists of four main pillars.

First, my recovery will be a lifelong endeavor, not necessarily because I will struggle every day with bingeing or purging or restricting or judgmental thoughts, but because I choose to make it so. I choose to wake up and recognize that my life as it is would not be if not for the recovery from the eating disorder. Allowing myself to fully experience life started with the practices I learned through therapy: nutritional guidance, self-reflection, and relationships. I choose to utilize these tools every day.

Second, I have chosen to join the helping profession as a social worker, psychotherapist, and advocate for those struggling with eating disorders. I have seen the power of treatment firsthand. Having the opportunity to provide these services to all people—

no matter their color, gender, sexual orientation, or age—
struggling with their relationship with food and how they may
feel about their body will be the privilege of my life.

Third, I have chosen to forgive and let go. I forgive myself, I
forgive my parents, and I forgive those who did not recognize a
boy in trouble. None of it was ever intentional.

Mostly, though, my recovery is about giving myself permission. I
give myself permission to feel worthy; to be sick; to want help;
to cry; to feel happy; to seek therapy; to speak up; to take
breaks (and naps!); to make mistakes; to learn; to protest; to
write; to practice spirituality; to love my culture; to love my
parents; to be proud of what I look like; to work hard; to be big;
to be small; to be healthy as I define it; to eat; and to take up as
much space as I need in this world.

I hope everyone who reads this essay gives themselves
permission for all of this and more. Take as much time as you
need to find a way to allow yourself to not only be in this world
but to thrive in it. It took me—and is continuing to take me—
years. The wait and the work are worth it.

I finish my story with one final journal entry, a cliché of epic
proportion: One truth, I suppose, is that I must learn to love
myself. Most days I do, and it is the best relationship I'll ever
have.

*Prior to joining the ranks of licensed social workers, Francis
worked under President Barack Obama in the United States
Department of the Interior and the United States Department of
Energy, as a political appointee in the Office of the Secretary.
Upon departing Washington, D.C. in 2016, Francis enrolled in
the University of Pennsylvania's School of Social Policy and*

Practice, where he received a master's degree in Social Work. He looks to continue his clinical work as a psychotherapist focusing on treating and advocating for individuals struggling with disordered eating, body image, eating and feeding disorders, and associated mental health challenges.

I have now realized there is something much greater in control of my life. Having control still brings a feeling of stability, but knowing I can only control certain things, like my perspectives and my reactions, really helps me maintain my emotions and overcome this disorder.

—Piper Indigofera

Limiting Behavior

Piper Indigofera

From early on I developed confusing thoughts about food. My parents' marriage was failing, and they had very different approaches to feeding me. I'm told my mother fed me a certain amount and then would give me more after a while. My father, on the other hand, would feed me a whole bottle or jar of baby food and then give me another if I did not slow down eating. I would usually end up vomiting from an over-full stomach.

As I got older, my parents and grandparents would always stress finishing my food and remind me that there were people starving in other places. I felt I had to eat more food than I wanted so that it did not go to waste. I ended up always eating what was in front of me on my plate, whether I wanted it or not.

I was also more concerned with other people than I was myself. My internal vision of what I thought I looked like was not what I saw in the mirror, even during my preschool years.

When I was in first grade, I moved to a different school. I had never enjoyed eating breakfast or even getting up to ensure I would eat breakfast, so I would usually go without. I would go to a babysitter's and eat an afterschool snack. I would then eat a big dinner with my mom after we got home.

I hit puberty by third grade and had put on a lot of weight from the stress of moving to a new school. I physically felt different from all the other kids at my school. By fifth grade, I was isolating myself a lot more and eating a whole, normal-sized, bag of doritos as a "snack." I began receiving more comments from my family members about how I was becoming overweight. Even the doctor said I was on the edge of being considered overweight for my height and age.

The comments about my weight from all these people were difficult to ignore, and they carried over into school because no boys seemed interested in me. I began working out daily and talking with girlfriends about exercise routines. My mom encouraged this in me and invited me to weigh in weekly with her.

By sixth grade I became obsessed with the number on the scale and the number of my jean size. I was even obsessed with the letter size of my shirt. I was offended if a family member gave me a top that was "too big." I began wearing skin-tight clothes so that I could wear a smaller size and feel more confident about myself.

When I started losing weight around this time, my family and I would go shopping every weekend. Pounds were melting off of me, and it felt good to have new clothes all the time. Without the clothes on, though, I could never look at myself in the mirror. I wanted to look like other people, and I wanted to be pleasing to them. I felt like if I could be somewhat attractive to others, then I could also be attractive in my own eyes.

Since I was not feeling attractive in my day-to-day life, I began looking online for male attention. Friends showed me different websites to visit to meet people, and one even gave me a webcam. I began trying to please people on these websites, particularly males.

I would give these men whatever they wanted as long as they told me how attractive I was. If they said any negative comments I could just block them or leave the conversation. I talked to many people from many different parts of the world and became attached to a lot of them because of the attention I got from them.

Eventually, my mom found out what I was doing and prevented me from meeting men online. Shortly after this time, in 8th grade, I began limiting my food intake and would only eat dinner with my mom and family so that they had no idea what I was doing to myself.

By doing this I finally got down to my goal weight. Family told me how beautiful I was again and commented on how much weight I had lost. I even got down to my goal jean size, even though I barely fit into them. I actually began looking at myself in the mirror, but I still only looked at my flaws. I never actually got to "enjoy" being at my goal weight.

After a few months of this, I began to feel hunger again. I ate significantly less, though, because my stomach had naturally shrunk. I felt I had more control over my eating at this point. At the same time, I was starting to feel fewer emotions, which caused other behavioral problems as well.

By my freshman year of high school, I was still exercising daily and trying to get a boyfriend. I achieved that halfway through the year, although, ironically, he was dating someone online while he was dating me and left me early in our relationship because of it.

A couple months after that, I met my highschool sweetheart. I finally felt complete in my social life and like all my hard work had paid off. He came from a matriarchal Italian family, and Italian women love to cook and feed their guests. I now had access to some of the best made-from-scratch foods ever: pizza, pasta, sauces, casseroles, garlic bread, cheesecake, cookies, etc. I loved it all and ate until I was overstuffed because I felt I finally deserved such delicious food after all my hard work.

After a little over a year of dating him, I had gained 30 pounds. I had stopped weighing myself for a while, and when I re-weighed myself I was shocked. Our relationship was great in the beginning, but by this time we had avoided any potential conflicts and were unaware of our internal emotions and how they were influencing our relationship. I know I was definitely eating my emotions in this relationship.

My boyfriend and I began to work out together, but we had differing ideas of working out; he wanted to get bigger muscles, and I wanted to get lean. This caused some slow-building tension in our relationship. I began feeling less attractive no matter how much he would tell me how beautiful I was. Being told I was beautiful only went so far for me since I had a predetermined image of myself in my mind that did not match reality.

I began limiting my eating again, but only by eating smaller portions. I did this in combination with an exercise regimen, and I got down to what I considered a "healthy" weight for my body. I still felt this underlying sense of depression and anxiety, though. I felt as though I was a victim of what I ingested. Limiting this stuff and taking pills to attempt to lose weight only helped so much with my idea of where I should be physically.

I came to terms with the fact I could never get down to my goal weight ever. I realized it was unrealistic for my body type. I had built up so much muscle from lifting weights and body exercises that my muscle exceeded the amount of fat I could burn in my body. This is how I rationalized it for myself so I could deal with the numbers I saw on the scale and with how physically strong I am compared with other women my age.

After seven years, just as I graduated college, I found out my boyfriend had cheated on me and had lied to me about it while also keeping other aspects of his life secret. It was a difficult decision for me to leave him, but I ultimately decided honesty and communication were more important to me in an intimate relationship than the time invested into it. The following two weeks were very depressing for me, especially because it was Christmastime.

I was so depressed I had no appetite for all the Christmas food. I had to force myself to eat at family gatherings, but I ate a small amount. That small amount made me feel overstuffed. During that time if I did not distract myself, I was bawling my eyes out. Food became somewhat of a distraction for me.

My other distractions were, again, talking to people, mainly men, online. I came back to what I knew. Though this time I was able to meet people who were in my area, and I ended up meeting my life partner. These things perked up my self-esteem and eliminated my concerns about what size I was or how much I weighed.

My partner is a cook, so food is part of his everyday life. His modeling of healthy eating and coping methods has helped me increase the emotional support I provide within myself. He gives me a healthy space to help me realize my emotions and confronts them with me. He points out when I am "eating my feelings" instead of eating for energy and nutrients. I feel emotionally supported by him in a way that no one else has ever been able to do. This strong emotional support gives me the ability to feel I can control more of how I react to situations. He forces me to confront my emotions and gives me potential solutions to my emotional complaints.

In my experience, eating disorders are an internal, learned response to the environment around an individual. For me, it was all about control. If I could limit my eating, I could control more in my life, including my emotions. I have now realized there is something much greater in control of my life. Having control still brings a feeling of stability, but knowing I can only control certain things, like my perspectives and my reactions, really helps me maintain my emotions and overcome this disorder.

I felt like emotional support was lacking when I was a child; it might have been shoved aside for more physical support like food or physical comfort. Feeling a sense of control, connection, and emotional support has been the best thing in my recovery from my eating disorder. The disorder will always be there, like an addiction, but being supported in the ways I need helps me stay healthy. Keeping a neutral realistic perspective is also helpful.

One way I support myself is through using a journal. Journaling has helped me with the emotional and mental side of this disorder. That along with meditational awareness has allowed me to realize that I physically compare myself to almost every other woman I come into contact with. This is the next step in the recovery process for me: ending the comparisons and beginning to empower other women within my life. I also need to work on forgiving myself.

I now know that abstinence is about much, much more than pursuit of a certain weight or body type. It's about being the best person I can be so I can help other people. It's about being present in my life instead of obsessed with food and weight and fat.

—Sarah

Wanting More

Sarah

Hi, my name is Sarah, and I'm 43 years old. Here are some things that are true about me: I'm a mother, a wife, a corporate executive, and a writer. I am also a compulsive eater who binged, starved, overate, and dieted for most of my life, until three years ago when I started a recovery program for my eating disorders. I want to tell my story in order to share my strength and hope with others who may still be struggling.

My earliest memories are of wanting more, of furtive delight in an unexpected treat, of sneaking and hiding food, of knowing I wanted more than I *should* want, more than other kids wanted. So while events in my life have made me turn to both bingeing and restricting, the disease began percolating at a very young age, probably part nature and part nurture. My mother and sisters have this disease, so maybe there is some genetic component, but I was also raised in a house that equated food with love and rewards.

I don't remember what I was for Halloween most years, and I don't remember the excitement of choosing and making a costume. I remember only candy—the effort to acquire and eat as much as possible and feeling angry at my parents if they made us call it a night before I had collected what I thought was "enough." There was never enough. I snuck extra, stealing from my sisters and the candy we gave out at our house so my own stash would last longer. Of course it didn't last—friends at school were still dipping into theirs weeks after mine was long gone.

I also stole money from my mother. From a very young age, I was allowed to ride my bike alone to a nearby convenience store, and I took change and dollar bills from my mother's purse to buy candy and chips, foods that were forbidden at home. I would eat them in secret on the way home, stuffing my cheeks and eating as quickly as possible. I knew my appetites were unusual and needed to be hidden. All the kids my age liked sweets and wanted treats, but they'd get full or sick to their stomachs long before I would. I knew I was different—I never stopped eating just because my stomach hurt.

I got the message that an appetite and a large body were to be hidden and ashamed of from my mother, who had a weight problem all her life. When I was small, our family ate healthy food at meals, but I regularly caught my mom with her own stash of candy or ice cream that she didn't want to share.

When we were sick or sad, we were comforted with food, whatever we wanted. When I was home from school, I got to watch Donohue with my mom while she folded or ironed, and I ate and ate and ate with no judgment or hiding. It was safe and cozy and lovely to be the only kid at home with her, snuggled on the couch with treats and rare parental attention.

My childhood was, on its surface, happy. Underneath the facade we presented to the world, however, my mother was extremely depressed, and my father had an anger problem. It turned out he was hiding a secret life we wouldn't find out about until I was in college. But there wasn't an excessive amount of fighting or yelling. We had plenty to eat, and we went to good schools.

I wasn't fat as a kid despite all my bingeing—I must have been active enough. I was solid and strong. Pictures of my elementary-school years don't show a willowy child, the way so many girls are at that age, but I was far from overweight. I was not aware of my body as good or bad until fourth grade, when a friend's mother told us all to suck in our tummies while we waited in line for a slide at a water park. I was horrified. It had never occurred to me to hide my stomach, but I took it as gospel after that.

Bulimia and anorexia started to affect classmates in my middle school. I tried both, but they didn't take hold. I remember one girl fainted in health class because she hadn't eaten in a few days, and I was so jealous of her willpower and strength.

Babysitting introduced a new world of food sneaking and binge eating. If the house where I was babysitting had any good food, I would put the kids to bed as early as possible and eat as much as I thought I could get away with. One of the families had big, Costco-size boxes of 500 mini York Peppermint Patties in their cabinet, and I would eat 20 or 30 or even 50 at a time, hiding the wrappers in the trash or taking them home with me, stopping only because I was on the verge of throwing up or was afraid my theft would be noticed. The houses that didn't have candy usually at least had chocolate chips in their baking cabinet. I never drank their booze or had boyfriends over. I only ate.

The summer between 8th and 9th grade, when I was 14, I was sexually assaulted on a date with an 18-year old boy I hadn't told my parents about. I didn't know at the time it was assault; I thought I was an idiot for being alone with him and that it was my fault, or that I'd been "asking for it." Most of the therapists I've seen have connected this early betrayal of trust to my weight and body issues; the theory is that women put on weight to avoid attention and keep themselves safe. I suppose there is something to that, but it's never done me much good to spend a lot of time looking at the "why" of my eating disorder. Since I was very young, I have eaten when feeling anything: good, bad, bored, sad, excited, nervous. I have eaten to numb myself and feel nothing. So sexual assault is part of my eating disorder story, but it's not my whole story.

My compulsive overeating really took off with the acquisition of a part-time job and a car at age 16. My part-time job was in an ice cream shop, and I ate pounds and pounds of the stuff whenever the store was empty. I ate low-fat and fat-free ice cream, of course, because a half gallon of low-fat ice cream was "diet food" in my universe, especially when paired with a low-calorie soda. Often I would go straight for the toppings. I could eat four or five whole candy bars while prepping toppings, and no one would be the wiser.

My other big habit in high school was to binge when I was studying for exams. I would buy an entire bag of cookies or a pound of candy when I had a test or paper to write, and I would eat while I studied. Between work and studying, I ate until I felt sick and comatose at least three or four times a week. Sugar made up most of my calories during this time. We always ate dinner together as a family, but I would often skip breakfast and lunch, eat a healthy dinner, and then binge all night. No one knew.

My weight was fairly stable during high school. I was not a waif, but I wasn't fat. When I look at pictures of myself from ages 13 to 18, I see a soft, curvy, beautiful girl. In my head, I was repulsive and horrifically overweight, a total failure in life despite good grades, a job, and an active social life. I felt like I took up too much space in the world and that no boy would ever want me. When I was rejected for anything, I assumed it was because of my weight, so I never considered that any other part of my personality or character could be problematic or off-putting.

Freshman year of college, away from home and knowing no one, I was so depressed, I stopped eating and lost weight—the only time I have reacted to depression in this way in my life. I often got so hungry that I was shaky and nauseous, and hunger made me feel virtuous and noble. I loved the asceticism of it, the denial. It made me feel powerful and like I had finally gotten control of my appetites. This was my first experience with restricting. It didn't feel like a choice or a desire to lose weight, though I liked that side effect. It lasted all of freshman year, until I fell in love.

The summer after freshman year, I started dating the man who is now my husband, my dad came out of the closet, my parents split up, my sister had a nervous breakdown, and my other sister got arrested.

I was keeping it together at school and helping out at home, but the next three years of college were marked by total out-of-control bingeing and a significant weight gain that stayed with me on and off until about three years ago. I ate sugar all day every day, with almost no healthy food. I felt tired and depressed all the time. I started to have anxiety attacks when I had sex with my boyfriend. I did not connect any of these events with the way I was eating. I looked at eating as a way to cope with all these horrible things, not as a potential cause of the feeling that I was spiralling out of control.

My boyfriend's mom lost weight at Weight Watchers, and I decided to follow in her footsteps. At age 23, I lost weight and started to feel better about my body. I couldn't believe it, though, when instant happiness didn't follow in all other areas of life: I was still having problems with my boyfriend, I was still having anxiety attacks, and I was feeling totally unfulfilled by my first job out of college.

Nothing was ever enough for me—not enough money, not enough love, not enough cigarettes, not enough admiration, not enough weight loss. I thought if I lost more weight it would solve all my problems. I was obsessed with counting points and gaming the system to eat things that were point-free, exercising to earn more points, and alternatively bingeing and starving. I thought about food all day. I developed lots of weird rituals to make food last longer and preferred to eat foods where I could get a lot of volume. I felt like I'd lucked into a program that would allow me to keep eating like I wanted while still losing weight.

From ages 23-27, I kept my weight relatively normal through alternating bingeing, starving, and compulsively exercising for hours each day. I moved to a big city, had adventures, got promoted, got married. I thought I had the weight problem solved, even if I still thought about my body all day. But after a miscarriage and then a full-term pregnancy at age 28, I found myself with a husband, a full-time job, and a baby, and I just couldn't stop overeating. After my son was born, when most women lose weight, I gained weight and kept on gaining.

For the next 11 years, from ages 28-39, I tried Weight Watchers a dozen or more times. I severely restricted calories. I did triathlons; I tried exercising four hours a day. I tried over 40 diets, some of which worked, many of which mimicked anorexia under the guise of a diet plan. I tried "intuitive eating." I bought more than 20 self-help books about dieting. I did therapy, both alone and with my husband. I saw a therapist specifically for food and weight issues. I wrote down my feelings, and I worked to heal from sexual trauma. I took baths and drank tea and meditated; none of it ever worked for long. I had another baby and worried I wouldn't have a low-risk pregnancy and natural delivery because of my weight.

I have lost 50 pounds three times. I have lost 20 pounds at least a dozen times. It wasn't at all unusual for me to start a new diet and lose 15-20 pounds in a month or two. It always came back, with a few more pounds than I'd lost each time.

In 2015, I turned 39 years old and had a turning point that changed my life, hopefully forever. I was at my heaviest weight and was desperate not to be fat at 40. I wasn't focused on improving the quality of my home life, sanity, marriage, or work; I focused only on wanting to be thin. I resolved to bring all my willpower and dieting experience to bear and started dieting over and over again.

I tried every diet that had worked for me in the past, and for the first time in my life, I couldn't string two days together. I would starve until 4 pm and then binge so much I was too full to eat dinner with my family. Or I would start a fresh diet on Monday morning and by Tuesday mid-morning, I'd run to a convenience store to buy donuts. None of the diets that had worked before worked for me now. It was because I was almost 40 and had a bad metabolism! It was because I hated my job! It was because I had a genetic predisposition to fatness! I just could not lose even a single pound.

That summer after a solid six months of trying and failing to diet, I began to read every weight loss memoir I could find from the library. I read about surgery, calorie restriction, hypnosis, exercise, self actualization.

Finally, as I lay on the beach one day with my family in an old-lady swimsuit that covered up the body I had always considered hideous, I read a book about Overeaters Anonymous (*Passing for Thin: Losing Half my Weight and Finding Myself* by Frances Kuffel), and a light bulb went off. Finally an approach that addressed what I had begun to think of as my addiction to certain foods.

I went to my first meeting a week later in August of 2015, and I was terrified. Something in me knew this was different, that it wasn't a lark that I'd try and then reject. I was expecting a huge room of people where I could disappear and hide in the back, the way A.A. is depicted in movies. But there were six or seven people sitting in a circle when I arrived, and they welcomed me to sit in the circle with them. I eyed them critically—some were fat, some were thin. What could these people possibly teach me? The thin people wouldn't understand me, and the fat people didn't have any help for me.

But I sat down and listened as they read from a book and shared. I cried on and off through the whole meeting. These people were sharing—and laughing??—about the topics I found most shameful and secret in my life. Even my husband and closest friends had no idea how much I hated my body and just how much I ate.

The people in that room talked about hiding and stealing food, binge eating in secret, eating from the trash, vowing over and over again to lose weight and being unable to do it. I was pretty sure I'd found my tribe. They also talked about what they'd done to get over those behaviors, but I didn't listen to that part. I was so overwhelmed by hearing what they'd done in their disease. I had always thought I was the only one.

After the meeting, an older woman came over to hug me—
which I hated! She said, "I hope to see you again tomorrow!"
Tomorrow? I'd never gone more than once a week to any
weight loss group before!

That afternoon I got a text from one of the thin, beautiful
women in the group just saying hello and that she hoped she
would see me again. She didn't ask me what I was eating that
day, what I weighed, what my plan was. Just a gentle welcome
and encouragement to keep coming back.

I did keep coming back. OA recommends you go to six meetings
before deciding whether it's for you, and that's what I did. Every
other "diet" I've ever done, I've thrown myself into 150% on day
one and then fizzled out after a while. Somehow I knew OA
would be different, and I knew I should shut up and learn before
I did anything. I bought a book or two but didn't change the way
I was eating right away. I think I wanted to hang on to my crutch
as long as I could. Most of all, I wanted the thinness that some
of these people had, but I also started to want the serenity and
peace they had around food and their bodies (as they say,
"come for the vanity, stay for the sanity!").

About five years before finding OA, I had read a book called
Drinking: A Love Story by Caroline Knapp, a recovering alcoholic.
She described her love affair with alcohol and her efforts to give
it up despite the intensity of her feelings. She shared stories
that were so familiar to me I could have written them, only I'd
done them with food, not booze. She hid bottles around the
house, as I'd done with food. She polished off half-full bottles,
only to replace them and drink the new one down to the same
level, which I'd done with ice cream. She lied to everyone about
how much she drank. I was reading my story, and it planted a

seed that perhaps I was addicted to sweets the way she was addicted to alcohol.

Receptive to the idea of food addiction, I gradually began asking people how to get started. One young woman told me to make a list of red light, yellow light, and green light foods. Red light foods were those that always gave me trouble and yellow light foods were those that sometimes gave me trouble. Green light foods were things I could always eat safely. My red light foods were all sweets. I was encouraged to start with giving up sugar.

I planned an epic, three-day binge and had a date in mind for giving up sugar: August 19, 2015. The date was planned around a dinner party given by a dear friend who excels at making desserts. I figured I would finish with a bang, eat myself into a coma, and get abstinent the following day.

I woke up on August 18 feeling sick and sluggish, and a tiny thought wormed its way into my head. What if I gave up sugar today instead of waiting until tomorrow? What if I just skipped dessert at the dinner party? I don't know where that thought came from, but I did it, and that was my first day without sugar (I gave up alcohol too). I haven't had any sugar or alcohol since August 18, 2015, more than three years ago.

Giving up sugar was hard but not impossible. I had a lot of support from people in OA, and I mainlined OA podcasts and reading material the way I used to mainline candy and baked goods. I still ate whatever I wanted whenever I wanted—chips, sandwiches, huge portions of anything that didn't have sugar in the first four ingredients.

Gradually, I started to want more of the program the way I'd once wanted more food. I knew I had to eventually get a sponsor, but I was suspicious. Frankly, OA seemed like sort of a cult to me. Everyone used the same terminology, chanted the same prayers, and talked about God all the time. I considered myself agnostic. If there was a power greater than me, and maybe there was, surely he or she had more important things to do than help me get skinny.

I called a friend who'd been in A.A. a long time and asked, "How do I choose a sponsor?" She answered wryly, "You're not gonna like this one bit, but I suggest you pray about it. Then you ask them to be a temporary sponsor so you can feel each other out and see if it works."

She was right; I didn't like it, but rolling my eyes the entire time, I asked God for a sponsor who was my age, thin, beautiful, married with children, a working mom (preferably a businesswoman), and non-religious. A name instantly popped in my head: Anne. I shook my head, no. Anne was in her mid-80's, not married as far as I could tell, and she was a normal weight but not super skinny. She was kind and gentle and loving but not what I was looking for. So I asked again, and Anne kept coming to mind.

Another prayer given to me by my friend in A.A. was this: "God, please hit me over the head with a 2x4. Make your will very obvious to me, because I am very slow."

The next morning, less than 12 hours after my prayer, Anne called and asked for a ride to the meeting because she doesn't drive. I thought, *Okay, okay, I get it, God . . . or whoever you are. I'll give Anne a try.*

The day I drove her to the meeting, I worked up the nerve to ask her to be my temporary sponsor. Over the course of the conversation, I learned that she was a nun. So in my quest for a young, married, non-religious, working mother, I ended up with a sponsor who was 86, single, childless, retired, and a Catholic nun.

The whole thing was funny actually. Any higher power of mine would have to have a sense of humor to get through to me, so I thought, *Good one, God. IF you even exist.*

Anne was just what I needed as a newcomer. She taught me gentleness. As I tightened up my program and had slips along the way, she would say with genuine love and affection, "Congratulations! This is wonderful news. God is reminding you of step one, that you are powerless over food." I despaired over any perceived imperfections, but she delighted in them as a direct message from God. I told her I had to beat up on myself or I'd get too lazy, and her response was, "Well, how has that worked for you so far?" She encouraged me to experiment with being as kind and loving to myself when I screwed up as I would be to a beloved child or elderly relative.

For a while, Anne was my higher power—a symbol of unconditional love and acceptance no matter how fat I was, no matter how much I ate, no matter how much of a screw up I was. She always took my call no matter how bad my day had been, which became a powerful metaphor for what I needed a higher power to do. She was also the first person in my entire life who knew what I did with food.

Over the first six months, my food plan evolved as I achieved weight loss and serenity and wanted more. For a while, I was counting days of abstinence, but I would have a slip on day 29 or day 59. It was clear I was self-sabotaging myself. I complained to an OA friend one day how frustrated I was to start back at day 1 again. She said, "We ALL only have one day. The person in the room with the most abstinence is the person who woke up the earliest. You have to take this one day at a time." I stopped counting days, steps, calories. Counting anything, it turns out, makes me crazy.

I should pause to say that eating plans are very individualized in OA. The program itself doesn't recommend one plan. Many people give up sugar and flour, but not everyone does. Some people snack, some don't. Some weigh and measure, some don't. It's a matter of working with your sponsor, your higher power, and sometimes a professional nutritionist to find out what works for you. We all have different flavors of this disease, and my abstinence could kill you and yours could kill me.

After six months or so, and motivated solely by a desire to lose more weight faster, I went to see a local nutritionist who suggested I measure my portions and cut back my calories significantly. I'd noticed a lot of people in OA with great recovery that weighed and measured their food, so I decided to give it a try.

It made me totally fucking crazy. I started losing weight, and it turns out I am as addicted to and compulsive about weight loss as I am about food. I alternated overeating and undereating, I was compulsively weighing, and I thought about food and my body all the time.

It occured to me this was not a sane response. I had lost weight, but I felt crazier than ever.

At that point, I started to realize dieting was as big a problem for me as overeating. My husband confessed that he was on the verge of staging an intervention for my dieting during this time in OA. He said, "I don't know why you think you're an overeater anyway...you eat a little too much on Thanksgiving and Christmas, but you just have a slow metabolism."

Bless his heart. He'd never seen me eat—I did it in secret.

In conjunction with a sponsor, I fired the nutritionist and went back to the food plan that worked best for me at that time, which was three meals a day, no snacks, no seconds, no sugar and no alcohol. This worked for me for many months. I maintained my weight loss but didn't lose any more. Eventually, I got frustrated.

Every time I have cut something from my food plan motivated by a desire to lose weight, it has backfired on me. Every time I have made a change motivated by a desire for more sanity, it has worked. Interestingly enough, just recently I went back to a weighed and measured food plan, but this time it was motivated by quieting the food thoughts in my head rather than by a desire to lose more weight. I don't know if it will keep working forever, but I know that just for today, it is.

Fast forward to three years into the OA program. I am maintaining a healthy weight. I have peace around my body image. I don't hate myself. This is a miracle beyond any that I could have imagined, and in many ways, body acceptance has been more important to me than weight loss. In a meeting last summer, someone who looked like me shared that she wore a bikini to the pool, and I gasped internally and thought, *Wait, hold the phone! Are people who look like us allowed to wear bikinis?*

I decided that not only was I allowed to wear a bikini at my age and size but that if I didn't wear one, I was letting the patriarchy win. If you'd told me five years ago that I would be at peace with my body and wearing a bikini to the pool with all the other suburban moms, I would have called you a liar. But I do it, and it feels great. This is a miracle for someone who has spent as much time hating their body as I have.

My food plan has changed a lot over the years, and I've had some leaps forward and some setbacks. A sponsor helped me determine that caffeine and artificial sugars are triggers for me, so I gave those up. I noticed that I do okay with potato chips and french fries, but I just can't stop with tortilla chips, so I gave those up (my food plan calls for no "recreational corn," which is embarrassingly silly but works for me). I try to use peace of mind rather than weight as a goal, so when I'm deciding if I will eat something or not, I ask, *Will this bring me closer to or further from peace?* I no longer ask if it will bring me closer to or further from my fantasy size.

This is a full-scale peaceful revolution inside my head and my heart.

A few words on God. Early on in the program, I refused to say the prayers because I didn't believe them and didn't want to be a hypocrite. I was desperate enough to keep coming to meetings but found myself rolling my eyes when people talked about relying on God. If (and that's a big if) there was a higher power, it certainly wasn't interested in me and should direct its attention to war and famine.

Then someone shared at a meeting that they'd gone to the ocean and tried to make the tide come in and failed. They'd commanded the sun to rise, and it hadn't. They had to admit there was a power bigger than them, even if it was science or nature or gravity. Another person shared that food was clearly stronger than they were, meaning food was a higher power of sorts. I related to that and realized if food was stronger than me, I needed something stronger than it.

Something slowly shifted in me, and I decided I didn't have to figure it all out. One afternoon after months of trying to get clarity, I had an image of God—a grandmother tree, old and wizened, who loves every single thing about me like a good grandmother does, but who will tell me the truth—with compassion—when I fuck up. She does not cause bad things to happen in the world—she cries when people starve or hurt each other. She wants the very best for me.

We hear a lot in the program that we should "turn it over to God," and what that looks like for me is a very short meditation where I imagine taking the thing I'm worried about (my body image, my marriage, my son's anxiety, my job, whatever) and wrapping it up in a blanket and handing it over to her. She cradles it and keeps it safe so I don't have to hold it anymore. She takes it from me, so that even if it still exists as a presence in my life, it isn't so heavy, and I'm not carrying it alone.

Coming to terms with a power greater than myself has been an integral part of my program. Sometimes I can't summon up any real faith, and the best I can do is know that if there is a God, I'm not it. That seems to be enough.

OA teaches us to never give advice. All I can do is say what's worked for me, and anyone who wants what we have can do what we do.

Here's what I think I've done that's helped me over the last few years in OA: I took it slow. I've always had a sponsor. I've worked the steps three times in three years. I've made many of my amends (but not all of them). I sponsor other people. I do service that requires me to be at meetings even when I don't want to go. I keep coming back and attend at least two meetings a week and often three or four. This has grown over time—my first few months in OA, all I did was go to meetings and allow people to care for me. You can start where you are and develop over time. I have wasted a lot of time wanting to do things as well and as spiritually as people who have been in the program for 20 years. My challenge has been to learn from those people but not hold myself up to their standard.

I've learned that I am a tremendously high-maintenance person. In order to stay sane and in recovery from my eating disorders, I need a lot of self care, including meetings, daily prayer and meditation, and sane exercise (I had to abstain from everything but walking for two years because I tend toward compulsive exercise). I need to pray and meditate every morning. I need more rest than I have ever been willing to admit to myself. I need to tell my sponsor what I'm eating every single day (I said I'd never do that, but I do now!). I need to be patient with myself and trust that my recovery will happen on God's timeline, not my timeline. I absolutely hate that, but I do better when I act as though I believe it.

Here's what I've done "wrong" in this program: take my will back approximately one million times per day, nurture petty resentments, pursue weight loss at the price of sanity, exercise all my character defects regularly and with enthusiasm, overeat even with abstinent foods, lie to my sponsor about what I've eaten, refuse to pray and meditate even when I know it helps me, decide over and over that I know more than everyone else in this program. However, I believe today that all my "mistakes" are not really mistakes at all; they're just my humanity keeping me humble and keeping me coming back. This program works via osmosis through the butt. Put your butt in a chair in a meeting, and the program will gradually start to work on you.

I now know that abstinence is about much, much more than pursuit of a certain weight or body type. It's about being the best person I can be so I can help other people. It's about being present in my life instead of obsessed with food and weight and fat. It's about snuggling with my husband in the evening instead of sending him away so I can eat in secret. It's about modeling for my children that it's safe to feel feelings, that we can survive and that it always, always, always gets better. If it doesn't feel better yet, I'm not at the end.

I'm not at the end of my eating disorder either. I consider myself recovering but not recovered. I haven't had a single day of starving or bingeing in three years that approaches anything like I did before, although I have still eaten too much or too little at times when my feelings just become too much for me.

I fully believe the A.A. adage that while I am in 12-step meetings in church basements, my disease is doing pushups out in the parking lot. I am convinced that even today, after three years without sugar, I could not have one bite of birthday cake without needing a whole piece and then two and then four, and then driving to 7-11 to buy ten candy bars, inhaling them, and then burying the wrappers at the bottom of the trash. That scenario is still in the realm of possibility for me.

My disease is one of extremes, of always wanting more and often taking less when it comes to food, sex, money, attention, and time. Working a 12-step program of recovery quiets the insatiable, critical voices in my head, one day at a time. Now when I want more, it's more peace and serenity. I never thought it was possible to have the freedom from food and body obsession I have today. I'm so grateful.

Sarah is a 43-year old technology executive living in Virginia with her husband and two kids. She attends three OA meetings a week, works the steps, and serves as a sponsor. You can get in touch with her by sending a message through the OA of Central Virginia Facebook page.

Families and Eating Disorder Recovery

Fear. Helplessness. Guilt.

These are the three emotions one mom describes feeling during her daughter's battle with anorexia. And this mom is not alone. Many family members whose loved ones develop eating disorders struggle to cope with their own emotions. They often feel overwhelmed with anxiety and fear while also worrying that they are in some way to blame for the problem.

At the same time, because many family members have never experienced an eating disorder before, they are unsure how to help. According to Deanna Linville, Ph.D., LMFT, Associate Professor of Marriage and Family Therapy at the University of Oregon and eating disorder specialist, "Researchers have demonstrated that often family and friends are confused about how to best support loved ones with an eating disorder and may unintentionally do or say things damaging in their attempt to be helpful."

Linville shares the following suggestions that can help family members provide the support their loved ones need:

- **Remember that the eating disorder is not your fault.** In her myth-busting presentation at the National Institute for Mental Health (NIMH) Alliance for Research Progress Winter Meeting, eating disorder specialist Cynthia Bulik, PhD, debunked the myth that families—and particularly moms—are to blame for eating disorders. "Moms have really taken the blame for anorexia nervosa, and we have to bust that myth because it's not true at all," Bulik says. According to Linville, "This does not mean that loved ones do not have a role in exacerbating the symptoms of an eating disorder or in supporting their loved ones toward and in recovery."

- **Separate the eating disorder from your loved one.** Know that the eating disorder may affect family dynamics and cause hurt. Keep in mind that your loved one cannot necessarily control the impact the disorder has on your relationship.
- **Team up with your loved one to conquer the eating disorder.** You can collaborate and work together toward recovery, figuring out the best way to support your loved one.
- **Model low anxiety around food, eating, and exercise.** Those impacted by eating disorders need to see how they can move forward toward a healthy relationship with food, eating, and exercise.
- **Model body acceptance.** Avoid making evaluative comments about weight and appearances that promote socio-culturally mediated images of attractiveness.
- **Know that it is normal to feel overwhelmed, sad, and anxious because of your loved one's eating disorder.** Reach out to your support network and consult a therapist if you need help coping with your own emotions.
- **Most importantly, provide love and warmth.** Consistently show your loved one how they can choose a path of health and eventually be free from their eating disorder. Show them that you love them by providing warmth and consistent support.

For more information on how families can support loved ones suffering from eating disorders, consult the Parent Toolkit created by the National Eating Disorders Association:

https://www.nationaleatingdisorders.org/sites/default/files/Toolkits/ParentToolkit.pdf

That was my turning point, learning there was a future for me, that if I could just manage to get over the rough moments there would be better waters in the future.

—Maya Levine

The Venn Diagram

Maya Levine

The Venn Diagram began to close sometime in August.

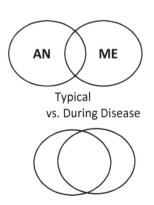

Typical
vs. During Disease

The **AN** stands either for **AN**orexia, or possibly for the initials of **A**norexia **N**ervosa. No one has ever told me despite all of the time I have spent looking at this damn Venn diagram. When I was taken into the hospital, they showed it to me. Every day in the hospital someone drew it without fail. Both of my therapists drew it for me regularly. I drew it myself trying to explain my disorder to a friend. Apparently, this Venn diagram explains how the entire process of the eating disorder works. The circles overlap more and more as you get deeper into the disease and begin to separate as you pull out of it.

My first therapist would not stop talking about how the me of the deepest disease had existed with a mind entirely eclipsed by the eating disorder. Some weird filmy haze covering my brain. Reverse mitosis, the two cells joining once more. Regression. No matter how many times the Venn Diagram was drawn for me, no one could explain how to separate the anorexia from myself. My thoughts were my thoughts. I couldn't tell what was supposed to be there and what wasn't, and no one would explain it. Every time I had a brief moment of what I suppose was clarity and thought, *maybe I shouldn't hate myself this much,* the thoughts poured back in like water out of a lock to say, *yes, you should.*

But where did all this hate, all this useless water, come from? The household I grew up in was mostly loving, and while there was conflict, it was always over in a few days. I had a set of friends I could depend on for support. I felt stress, yes, but I enjoyed my classes and activities. Even so, there were still strange, bubbling anxieties that swirled within me like the tide getting trapped by a set of rocks. They would rush in and then get trapped and fester and turn warm and grow moss. Maybe some of it came from the place. A Chicagoan born and raised, I moved to the health-crazed Palo Alto for high school, and by the time I was 16, fitting in seemed paramount. Surrounded by bodies thinner than mine, I found the need to change my own.

I once theorized in English class that when a teenager dealing with the complexities and injustices of first-world life experiences confusion and anxiety, the easiest target for those emotions is herself. She turns all the worry and rage inwards and tears down the foundations of who she is until she's standing on a rickety pile of pebbles. I stand by this theory, but now I believe that once the anger fills up that little tide pool, it spills back over and swamps the people that care about us the most.

As I ate less and less and exercised more and more, I felt relief. There was a cessation of the pressure. As my parents pushed me to eat, or offered to drive me places, or showed me care and love, I began to push them away. I became unfriendly. I closed myself off. I stayed away. I hurt them. The tide pool began to deepen, and then the water was dark and dingy and I couldn't see the bottom. I dove in and swam down. My clothes stopped fitting. I saw spots when I stood up.

Early in December 2017, things came to their breaking point. I saw two doctors and didn't think much of it. Then, during English class, I was removed from school. My parents informed me that I was going to be admitted to the hospital. I tried to play it off with a dark joke. They began to drive. I yelled at them. There was a look of pain on my father's face, but my mother kept going. I screamed that they were crazy, that they'd regret this when we all woke up tomorrow and I was still medically safe, as I believed I was at that moment.

We got onto the highway. I played my last card, breaking down in loud, heaving sobs at the unfairness of it all and the fear of going into the hospital and being forced to remain still, to eat, to stuff more and more into myself. I had had a plan for the night for what to eat and how to exercise. I remember it very distinctly. I remember how hot the tears were. I remember my mother's face wrinkling as she tried not to cry. I remember screaming, "You're wrong, you're wrong, I can't believe you'd do this, you know me. I wouldn't let myself develop anorexia!" I remember this because if they had turned around and taken me home from the hospital, I probably would have died that night.

I was in the hospital for twelve days. I hated it. I hated the smell, I hated the nurses, I hated being woken at 5:30 am to have blood drawn. I hated all of the food. I hated the support groups and Dialectical Behavior Therapy. I hated sitting in bed for twelve hours at a time.

My parents remained with me for all of it. They had work. The commute could be killer. I refused to let them sleep there. But no, they made the drive and took their work calls from the corner of my hospital room and were there so I didn't have to have my eating supervised by one of the nurses that I despised. They supported me. When I was falling, they were there to catch me. As I swam deeper and deeper, they grabbed me by the hair and dragged me back up, kicking and screaming. I was drowning and they saved me, and I hated them for it and made sure they knew it.

I screamed, "I hate you," as they coaxed me through another bite of bread, and I shouted that I despised them and wanted them to die as they continued to read through *The Old Gringo* in an attempt to distract me from eating. "I wish you would get out," I spat as they lobbied for my girlfriend to be able to visit me. They left my hospital room at 9:00 pm after my last meal of the day, and as they left there were words trapped in my throat, itching at my lips. I wanted to apologize, and I felt something deep and dark within me tearing me open, regret and pain and a wish for them to say they loved me, but I said nothing and they left to drive home in the dark and were there again before 8:00 am the next day to get me through breakfast.

I left the hospital, and the Venn diagram still felt like one circle. But I was medically stable, and now I could sleep in my own bed and breathe fresh air. My parents were there, and they dragged me home from school for meals and made me eat. I snapped pencils when the pressure got to be too much and stomped my foot and threw fits like a little baby. I felt childish, and I hated myself, but my little circle of rocks and sand couldn't hold all of the hatred, so I threw it outwards and made sure my mother took the brunt of it.

I think she complained twice. Twice, through all of that, only twice did she reprimand me for what I said. I don't think I've ever thanked her for that. I don't think I've ever said, "I see what you did and I appreciate it; I don't think there's a better mother in the world." I kept acting hateful. The rage abated as I settled into a routine and was able to leave my wheelchair and the food began to go down. The doctors told my parents I needed to eat more, and they complied. I fought. I yelled and sobbed. I ate. I hated.

Late in March, at midnight, I wrote them a letter. The poem spanned two pages. It was accusatory. It was visceral. It was wrong. Here is the last stanza:

Because roses are red

And violets are blue

Why do I feel this?

You know that it's you

It's you

It's you

It's you

And over and over until the page was filled with that single hateful phrase.

There was something that kept me from spilling out those simple words: "I was wrong. I love you." I feared that something horrible would happen to my parents before I managed to tell them I am sorry for the things I said and put them through. Perhaps I will show them this as a way of explaining the regret I feel.

As we lose control of our eating and our exercise, our negative emotions—our feelings about ourselves, our habits of comparing ourselves to others, our tendency to distort our bodies and minds so that we feel less, our hatred—grow, and we externalize that. Sometimes we cannot keep ourselves from saying things we regret. I'm not entirely sure controlling ourselves is always the right thing to do. Some things deserve to be said.

But they always need to be said along with an apology. When I feel there's no point in working to get better because I feel like there is no Venn Diagram—just a circle—when I fall back into my little tide pool and the urchins grow on me and the sand sharks eat away at my hands, when I am seized with the certainty that I will never not hate myself, I remember that I have not yet said I am sorry. And I work to get to the point where I can tell the people I love, the people that care about me the most, what I really feel, and try to make things right.

In June, a friend and I were walking home together and the topic of my eating disorder came up. She skirted the topic for a few moments before asking if I thought I was better. I told her I didn't know, that the hatred I felt for myself and the people around me certainly didn't make me feel like someone in a good place in their lives. I asked if she had even noticed that I had lost weight in the fall. She said she had and that she regretted not doing something sooner.

Then, around the anniversary of when I had stopped eating, I felt some satisfaction that I had managed to change myself. I also felt a much quieter emotion, much more benign. I felt a small bit of shame, of empathy for my friends and parents as they had watched me try to kill myself. I felt a small bit of release of the anxiety. The tide pool settled down. I bought some flowers on my way home and put them in water. I didn't tell my mother they were for her, but I think she knew. I hope she knew. The circles began to open.

The new school year began, and I went back to school. I ate lunch. I chafed at not being able to exercise, but I got through. I spent time with my friends and tried to stop pushing away people that just wanted to help me. I ate meals outside of the house without feeling much more than a stab of guilt. But I had the regular episodes of sobbing when I felt like I couldn't go on and was never going to get better. No one seemed to tell me when all of this would end, when I could go back to not eating six meals a day.

In September, my therapist announced that she had called in another one of her patients who had been in recovery for almost four years. She sent my parents out of the room and brought in the patient. I don't know what I was expecting, exactly, but I was caught off-guard by her large earrings and her red dress and the confident way she carried herself. She had been in recovery for almost four years. She was finishing college, enjoying her medical work, and thinking about where she might move when she was done with Stanford.

"You sound exactly like me," she told me after I ranted at her about how horrible the process was, how therapy was useless, how I wasn't getting better or if I was no one was acting like it. "I think I said things just like that when I was, what, a year out? And you're not wrong. And no, it still gets hard, but I can tell you that you *will* get over it. I still have to eat three meals, three snacks, but I don't beat myself up if I skip one or eat more than usual. I'm flexible. I make time in my life to eat and go to therapy and take care of myself." She went on to tell me more about her experience, the triggers, the process of getting over it.

She left the room, red dress floating out behind her over the threshold, and I was left feeling lighter than I had in months. I think that was my turning point, learning there was a future for me and that if I could just manage to get over the rough moments there would be better waters in the future. She seemed happy. I realized I was happy to have met her.

"Did you like talking with her?" my mother asked afterwards.

"Yeah," I said. "It was the greatest. Mom?"

She looked at me, and I tried to open my mouth to force out the words.

"I'm sorry," I finally managed. "For...everything." For the pain of watching me do this to myself and the effort required to help me get over it, for my ungratefulness and childishness, for the way I hadn't thanked her or apologized yet.

She shook her head. "It's okay. It's going to be okay." She reached out for my shoulder, squeezing it. "I love you, you know?"

"Yeah. I...love you too."

I felt light. I felt like my soul had been scrubbed clean. As we left the building, the circles felt distinct and the sun had never felt so warm.

Maya Levine was born and raised in Chicago and now lives in California. She has had work featured in Bluefire Magazine, the Palo Alto Weekly, Microcosms Online Contest, Roots Magazine, Enchanted Conversation, Zoetic Press, FurPlanet, MoonPark Review, *and* The Nature of Cities, *and has had a short play performed during Palo Alto Play Palooza. She has been in recovery for a year.*

I do still struggle, but I want life. It's not like I just want it. I'm proactively working for it.

—Anonymous

Wanting Life

Anonymous

When I was 11, unhealthy eating habits started to emerge; I remember trying to eat as little as possible. One summer, for instance, I was on vacation with one of my best friends. She was a model and always got attention, and she beat me at everything just a tiny bit. One night when we went out to eat we got hush puppies. We each got three, but something went through my mind: I decided I would eat a little less than her. Maybe that's how things started.

For most of my teenage years I didn't eat normally, but I didn't know what normal was. I was really big into sports, and long story short, I became very successful at running and diving.

When I was 16, I was raped by my friend's dad. At that time I struggled with drugs and alcohol. When I went to college, I struggled more with my eating disorder. I lost quite a bit of weight in a short amount of time. I was an athlete, so I went to a sports psychologist for help dealing with my eating disorder. He was really nice, but I fought recovery. I am the most stubborn person ever.

I ended up going to a special program for athletes with eating disorders. I did well, but I was a little rebel. For the next few years, I was constantly in and out of treatment. I was always sneaky.

Each time I relapsed, it got worse and worse, to the point where I couldn't even stand. I remember when I was bingeing and purging—it was the only time I could think about something without feeling. All I could focus on was the food, the physical experience.

The last two times I relapsed, it was horrible. I remember the only way I could survive was if I was bingeing and purging. I would pass out all the time, and I couldn't even lift my head.

My worst experience in treatment was at a place I still struggle to even say, so I call it the "C" word; those around me know what it is. It was the worst situation I've ever been in. It was so horrible I can't even think about it. It was a place for people with weight loss, for kids and teenagers, for behavioral kids, and for kids with medical challenges.

I was in the acute ward, and it was a nightmare. There were eight of us confined to a tiny room. I was spit on and called horrible, horrible names, and I had books thrown at me. I was punished for struggling. I hated everything about it, but it was the only place that would accept me because I wasn't stable enough for other centers.

I had always thought about ways to kill myself, to injure myself badly enough that I had to go to a real hospital. One time, I did hurt myself; the injury left a horrible yellow and green bruise the first few months I was there. The people at the center basically tried to sedate me, but I reacted strangely to the medication. I developed this horrible movement with my mouth I still sometimes do. I developed severe foot drop, and I couldn't stop rolling around crying and literally screaming. I truly couldn't stop.

After that, I went to another center. It wasn't my favorite treatment center, but it was the best for me. I don't really do well with lots of people also suffering from eating disorders, but many of the people there were dealing with substance abuse.

While I was there, I met a friend, my little angel, and she introduced me to God. I also had a really good friend who helped me develop a relationship with God, but this angel I saw every day for months. She helped me see who God is and not just what He does. She made me see how much He loves us and that nothing can separate that. I saw what joy and peace and gentleness my friend had. I found hope, and that was a big turning point for me.

From that point on, I have made constant efforts in recovery. Again, I do still struggle, but I want life. It's not like I just want it. I'm proactively working for it. I was at the last treatment center over two years ago. The longest I had gone out of treatment since age 18 was nine months, and it's now been a little over two years. Since then, I have sustained a job. I have totally surrendered myself to God. I was always a believer, but it used to be that when I struggled, I pushed myself away from God because I was doing horrible things. Now I have moved beyond that.

I've also gotten really into pet-sitting. I have always needed an identity. It used to be I was the runner and then the anorexic. Now I'm the pet-obsessed Jesus freak, and I love it. I have two Jack Russell terriers, and I spend time every day with the Bible. I walk every day because it helps me clear my mind, and it helps me eat well.

I've also been more open about how people can support me. My family is always a huge support. They don't always know how to help, but who can when you don't understand the struggles I face?

My dad has been the biggest support, in so many ways—not only in my eating disorder recovery—but in life in general. He gives me laughter, comfort, and so much more. 99.99% of the time I feel like a burden, but my dad always says a father wants to help his child. That helps me realize Jesus is our father and wants to give to us in a good way. I'm very blessed. I'm blessed to know Jesus, blessed He's used my struggles to hopefully share His love, blessed with people who care, blessed with the best two little dogs anyone could ask for, blessed to have hope, and blessed to be alive.

I've learned throughout this journey that I have to focus on my mental and emotional health. I try to put everything in perspective. If someone I love was struggling with something, I would feel so good if they came to me and I could help.

For the longest time I used my body, my emaciated state, to be my voice. To keep people away. To let them know they can't hurt me; only I can hurt me. For the longest time, I loved this whirlwind, but I hated the hurt it caused everyone. And my brain went back and forth between, *How dare I think I'm important enough to hurt anyone?* to just being so upset that they cared. I just wanted to go away.

I have changed. I have struggles, I have moments of self-hate, but I have Jesus and all the many blessings He's given me in abundance.

Truth is, I'm not purging anymore, but that doesn't mean I don't find myself ascending in a clickity-clackity coaster cart next to my feeble foreboding bully self again and again. What I do know is that, like the scores of other addicts who find the will to make better choices every day, I do, too.

—Terri Porter

Tipping Points

Terri Porter

I'm eating cereal with milk again. I haven't had a bowl in years because when I was at the height of my eating disorder that meant I'd rather purge than deal with my life.

Purging, although disgusting and inconvenient, made me feel magically capable of dealing with frustrations that had just moments before seemed insurmountable. I thought I was using it as a reset, a second chance to make better choices that tipped me towards my well-being and away from my illness, but instead I found myself stuck in a shameful loop on a merciless roller coaster. Every mechanical click, click, click that pulled me up, up, up was a painful reminder that I was going to be here—stuck—until I not only tipped, but leapt, tucked, and rolled away from purging and into dealing.

According to my mother, I didn't need rescuing. "You don't even look like you have an eating disorder," she claimed. She thought I didn't look the type. But had she known what to look for—and had I been willing to admit I had a problem—we could have ended the epic meltdown in a teary hug.

Instead, I isolated myself by saying nothing to anyone but my diary.

The Beginning

August 15, 1977. [11 years old] Today was my mom and dad's anniversary. I made a card and wrote a lot of poems for them. We fixed them breakfast in bed before my dad went to work.

There had been little need for a discussion about who would be responsible for what when my parents exchanged vows under a chuppah in 1959. Gerard agreed to be the handsome provider, and Vicki agreed to be the tight-cashmere-sweater-wearing beatnik who would raise their family.

Dad would already be long gone by the time my three sisters and I hit the breakfast table on Monday mornings. We'd grown accustomed to his nomadic life on the road as a traveling salesman Monday through Friday. We relied heavily on our stay-at-home mom, who handled the cooking, cleaning, PTA meetings, and homework assignments with all the magic of Mary Poppins, the humor of Lucille Ball, and the glamour of Elizabeth Taylor. She fed us with her life, and we were a hungry bunch.

Mom loved food. She didn't care so much for the mundane counting of calories or the achievement of following ambitious recipes. Instead, she poured her heart into making beautiful meals peppered with nuance. She considered a bowl of steaming pasta the perfect inspiration for conversation, and any type of pie was the cure for everything.

But her message about food was mixed: she loved to eat, but she was always on a diet, always a mere ten pounds away from the ideal body she imagined would help her live her best life. And while she harmlessly teased about wanting to be buried holding a fork and an extra strong Chinet plate—just in case heaven was BYO—her relationship with food affected my own and became as complex as my relationship with her.

September 4, 1977. [12 years old] Today I am having a friend sleep over. Her name is Lynn. We are having a lot of fun.
Goodnight, Terri

I joined the Girl Scouts of America with my new best friend, Lynn. After school on pigs-in-a-blanket and apple-brown-betty Wednesdays, Lynn and I would walk together to the church across the street where the Girl Scout meetings were held. Unlike Lynn, who wouldn't wear her uniform to school, I wore mine proudly and would have killed for the matching beret.

Lynn's mom, Sandy, was our Troop leader. She'd have Dixie cups of juice and badge-inspired activities ready to go upon hearing the heavy door announcing our arrival.

December 19, 1977. [12 years old] When I spend the night at Lynn's house please make all my worries go away. Also, I'm getting my hair cut tomorrow. Please help it look good or excellent! Thank you, Terri Porter

I'm excited about sleeping away because I know Lynn's family, yet I'm anxious because they are not my own family. And I worry. I worry because that's what I do at 12 years old, and then I reach out to the pages of my diary in the hope that getting it down on paper will bring me comfort and make all my worries go away.

When I arrive at the Kappes' for my overnight, Sandy welcomes me inside their log cabin, and her kind eyes put me immediately at ease. When Sandy extends an invitation for Mom to stay, I expect to hear, "Thanks, but..." and am surprised to hear, "Love to." She doesn't hold on to my neck as if to say, "Don't leave me alone with this person." Instead, I notice a subtle change in her tone—from normal to charming—as they launch into a dialogue and share a pitcher of iced tea even though my mother doesn't like iced tea.

January 16, 1979. [12 years old] Today we saw Ice Castles with Robby Benson! Mom and her friends went for a vacation. We got our Girl Scout cookie [order] sheets. Dad took one to his office and filled up half a sheet. I'm so happy.

Soon, although Mom still juggled the same exact schedule she claimed kept her from attending Girl Scout meetings, she was 100% on board to help me and my troop win the district-wide Girl Scout cookie order contest. I was thrilled to have her, but instead of basking in her attention, I watched Mom and Sandy become best friends. My undeveloped sixth sense was tugging on the skirt of my uniform as if to warn me that change was imminent. *You see what's happening, don't you,* it said in a sinister whisper. Annoyed and completely unprepared to question my mother or their relationship, I buried my concerns in my diary.

February 12, 1979. [12 years old] I feel all bunched-up with feelings and so let down. I want to get over it so badly. My dad is going to be gone all week and next week Mom's going to Des Moines with Sandy. I hope my parents still love each other very much.

Although we sold plenty of cookies, we did not win and were now faced with the obligatory task of delivering each box, but with Dad out of town on business and Mom off with Sandy, I was left with a bad combination of bunched up feelings and a hefty inventory of cookies.

February 23, 1979. [12 years old] Today I ate a whole box of assorted sandwich [cookies] and threw up. I have a headache.

February 28, 1979. [12 years old] Today they called off school so we stayed home and watched our soap operas. I am going to go on a diet. I weigh too much for a twelve-year-old.

Since I don't remember seeing examples of bulimia on television or in the movies, I don't know how I learned to purge or why writing no longer felt like enough. I was twelve years old and at my first tipping point when the part of my brain that saw everything as dark and foreboding went rogue and took over.

September 9, 1979. [13 years old] Today my mom and dad filed for a divorce. I cried very hard, and so did my dad. Tina is going with Mom, and I'm staying with Dad, Toni, and Tracy. We are all very sad.

The day Mom left us to be with Sandy, she said, "You already know and love Sandy." She was right. I loved Sandy. Then, looking into her rearview mirror, which she was using to apply the final coat of several shades of lipsticks, she added, "So take this time that I am giving you to get to know your father." Mom was always turning situations inside out, putting a positive spin on the most potentially distressing circumstances.

Sometimes I loved her for reminding me how to find the silver lining, but most of the time her comments just made me resent her for not acknowledging my feelings. Finally, she drove up the steep driveway with her arm hanging out the open window, her fingers lazily waving good-bye as she shouted, "I love you, my darlings. Call me." Left behind was a husband who was still in love with her and three daughters gasping for a hint of her Halston perfumed air.

September 10, 1979. [13 years old] Today in school I couldn't keep my mind on any subject. I hate it—living without Tina and Mommy. I just talked to my mom, and she keeps telling me she loves me. I love her. Everything is just a nightmare.

After she left, I felt as if I had been stripped of my identity because I had no experience at being anyone other than her loyal daughter. I was angry at Mom for putting me in this position. *What kind of mother would leave her children?* But I also felt confused and conflicted about my resentment. *What kind of daughter would stand in the way of her mother's happiness?* I was left to determine for myself: *Without her, who was I?*

August 10, 1980. I am fourteen now and really messed up! I went to [my friend] Angie's going-away party. Sean took me into a bedroom alone. He turned out the lights, and started pulling me down. I kept saying, "Forget it, Sean." Then he climbed on top of me and said over and over, "I want to make it with you." I kept saying no very loudly. Then he said, "Give me one good reason," and I said, "Me." He said, "That's not a good reason." So, I said, "If that's not a good enough reason—fuck you!"

The next night, before TV and after Dad attempted yet another microwave dinner recipe, I summoned the nerve to ambush him during dishes with a quick hug. In need of a connection I could trust, I wrapped my arms around his waist, buried my face in the back of his Oxford shirt that smelled of Old Spice and pipe tobacco, and gave him a good squeeze. Dad stood dumbfounded with his arms at his sides—a clear indication he didn't have a clue how to suddenly pivot from his role as provider to his new role as caretaker for three teenage girls. While I was in the act of hugging, I felt oddly fulfilled and inspired to keep trying to be closer until Dad took two steps backwards—away from me—and ambushed me right back.

September 9, 1980. [14 years old] Dad told us he's getting married.

I was immediately suspect of the pressed size-eight jeans my soon-to-be stepmother wore with pantyhose and her perfect blonde hair, which was somehow unaffected by humidity. My sisters and I hoped a freak storm would douse their outdoor ceremony and leave us without a stepmother and alone with the wedding cake; instead, the sun shone and vows were exchanged.

December 4, 1980. [14 years old] I am so fat for 5'2".

January 24, 1981. [14 years old] I gained most of the weight back that I lost last week, so tomorrow I start my diet again!

February 11, 1982. [15 years old] Today I passed out again at school from not eating and taking aspirins on an empty stomach. I make myself throw up sometimes when I've eaten too much junk or something. Nobody knows, but just because I passed out my stepmom thinks I have anorexia!

No matter how overwhelmed my new stepmom must have been with a new marriage, the challenge of suddenly raising daughters, her career, or her commitment to ironing and looking after my dad, nothing got past her. And while she thought she was being helpful in confronting me, our stepmother and daughter relationship wasn't capable of handling such a sensitive matter because our relationship completely lacked any closeness beyond mere proximity. So, when she knocked at my bedroom door late one night without her face on for a private chat, her monologue about the consequences of my self-sabotaging behavior didn't get past the black hole that separated us.

"Now, Terri," she said as she made herself comfortable on the edge of my bed, wearing her blue velour monogrammed robe with matching sash tied in a knot across her flat stomach, "Your father may not see everything that goes on around here, but I see what you're up to, and let me tell you..." At this point in her monologue, I stopped listening and simply took pleasure in watching the age lines around her mouth move as she spoke, still hoping for an "I'm not your mom, but I hope we can be friends" type of tender chat instead of this cold accusation. "Terri, you may be trying to hurt your father or your mother or me, but I'm telling you the only person that's going to get hurt by your destructive behaviors is you."

The Middle

Mom and Sandy welcomed all of us into their Buffalo Creek home, a one hundred-year-old cabin, for my older sister Toni's high school graduation party. There wasn't a seat to be had at the farm style table big enough for fourteen when the dark chocolate cake with buttercream frosting was ceremoniously served, so Tracy and I shared, shoulder to shoulder, cheek to cheek. As we pressed against one another, Sandy, who was standing behind me, put her hands on my shoulders.

"Ouch," I said and squirmed away from under her hands.

"Ouch what?" Sandy asked. "I was barely touching you. Hold still," she admonished, sharply turning me away from her, returning both hands to my collarbone, and walking her fingers right up onto the lump.

June 17, 1982. [15 years old] Mom immediately alerted Dad and then put me in the orange Subaru. We saw Dr. Levy.

At the doctor's office, there were no lights on over the receptionist's desk, no parents with sniveling children in the waiting room; everyone, including the doctor in his Sierra Trading Post pocket shorts, was in weekend mode. He didn't bother to put on his monogrammed doctor's coat before escorting us back to his office and flipping the switch to wake the fluorescent light over the examining table.

"How are you feeling?" Dr. Levy's soft-spoken inquiry seemed to calm Mom's frantic energy.

"Fine, I guess," I answered.

"Are you under a lot of stress at school?"

"Not really."

"What about at home?"

Well, I thought to myself, *that's a can of worms*, but when I opened my mouth, I answered, "No." After drawing a couple of vials of blood, Dr. Levy carefully taped a cotton ball over the puncture and assured us he'd get to the bottom of whatever this was.

"Well, what do you think it is?" Mom asked in a petulant tone.

"The lump could be a number of things," he explained in his best bedside manner. "We could be looking at Cat Scratch Fever, Mono, or Hodgkin's." Mom heaved a sigh and thanked Dr. Levy for seeing us on such short notice.

"What's Hodgkin's disease?" I asked on the long, winding ride home.

"Well, it's a form of cancer," Mom replied before raising her voice an octave and continuing in an English accent, "but we don't seem to really know anything yet, now do we?"

As if she wasn't acting strange and I hadn't just heard her say the word cancer, I changed the topic, "I hope they didn't finish the cake."

June 17, 1982. [15 years old] Visited Head of Hematology at Children's Hospital. I'm scared. They drew blood, measured me, weighed me, and checked my blood pressure (92/60). They took chest X-rays, found more lymph nodes around my lungs, and decided they should do a biopsy on me as soon as possible.

While my parents and I waited for the biopsy results in a private conference room, I calmly watched the clouds of a brewing storm gather over the mountains and resisted the urge to crawl between them and resume my childhood. What could I do, I wondered, to make this last?

June 17, 1982. [15 years old] At noon doctors told me it looked like Hodgkin's disease—cancer of the lymph nodes.

While everyone thought my cheery disposition made me the perfect candidate to fight the good fight against cancer, the truth is, from underneath the crisp cotton sheets of my hospital bed, despite the looming uncertainties facing me, fighting was the last thing on my mind. Suddenly unencumbered by my weight or the divorce, I was tucked in, surrounded by my once separated family, and perfectly willing to assume the role of doomed cancer patient.

For the next several days, Sandy documented all that was happening around and to me while I nodded in and out of consciousness:

June 23, 1982. At 12:45 the orderly came to take Terri down for surgery. Nurse Karen stopped to give her a Valium. She took it and said, "delicious blueberry pie." All the nurses turned around thinking someone had given her something to eat. She then proceeded to tell the orderly to "burn a little rubber" as he was pushing her down the hall. Her spirits were up, making it easier for all of us. That kid is something else.

June 24, 1982. You took the tube out of your nose, and that made you feel better. Visitors in and out all day. Results: No cancer from the diaphragm down. Oh, happy day. Shit on the Hodgkin's, but we are thankful it is nowhere else.

July 9, 1982. [15 years old] My operation was two weeks ago yesterday. Ready to start partying and enjoying my summer— not! My first chemotherapy was everything I didn't want—the pits! I threw up all day.

On the morning of my first chemo injection, hospital staff suggested that if I had a positive attitude I might not get sick. I accepted their challenge and focused on crushing the competition with all the vim and vigor of an aspiring cheerleader on tryout day.

The chemo moved through my veins just as I imagined a flame would travel down the wick to a readied stick of dynamite. I gripped the bed rail, rolled onto my side, and proceeded to vomit for the next eight hours. Certainly, a positive attitude can be good for a social life and for some types of healing, but spare me any rhetoric about using it to help fight the effects of a powerful drug combination. Mom climbed in bed and, from her spooned position behind me, held a pillow tight against my stitched-together abdomen. In her arms, I no longer felt like I was going to come apart. Her resilience cradled my vulnerabilities—in an instant, I was her child again.

Thanks to cancer, my fanciful dream of living with Mom once again came true. Cuddled on her porch, I watched the clouds shift, let the lilac-scented breeze seduce me in and out of sleep, and dreamt about how flat my stomach would look as I lay in a casket at my very tragic funeral.

December 28, 1982. [16 years old] I only have two treatments to go. I should be so happy. I just feel so different from everyone else.

I left the hospital flanked by family toting helium balloons and smiles and tears.

"Way to go, Paula," Toni teased, using one of our favorite lines from the scene when Paula was swept away from her miserable life by the handsome Zack Mayo in *An Officer and a Gentleman*. Strangers in the hospital lobby stood and clapped, and others lifted their arms victoriously, hooting and hollering. I watched the big eyes of kids in wheelchairs tethered to IV's, wearing bandannas and hats, as they looked at me with envy.

That night I dreamt I was a reluctant winner on the Game of Life show.

"Tell the survivor what she's won."

"Terri, you've won a brand-new life!"

But I didn't want it. Not only did I feel angry for being given more time, unworthy of this second-chance prize that other sick contestants had at the top of their wish lists, I also felt paralyzed with fear that I'd fail at living up to the expectations attached to being a teenage cancer survivor.

I didn't want bulimia to be the death of me, but I also didn't know how to live without an illness. I didn't know how to take the high road because every road I took felt like a detour. I was all over town, turned 'round, lost.

April [Undated], 1983. [16 years old] Was I so intimidating or unavailable that not one adult would want to take me in their arms and just rock me a bit instead of giving me the old pat on the back "get back into the game" speech? I was sixteen—didn't anybody see how scared I was?

May 30, 1983. [16 years old] People say we have to forget— there's no way I can or maybe I won't let myself. I don't know. All I do know is that cancer was an excuse to be held all day by her. Now I must move on and forget it ever happened—my life is not going to stop.

The summer before my senior year of high school, I was living back at Dad's house and thin—thanks to the chemo—when my slinking off after meals confirmed the return of my darkest foreboding.

September 3, 1983. [17 years old] On Saturday I woke up with a back and side-ache. I was on a terrible diet, but I felt fat! Mom was working hard for her big art show, where she sold out last year. Sunday I woke up, took a shower, ate breakfast, threw up, and went to Mom's show feeling very lightheaded. Then proceeded to my job.

Alone at my dad and stepmom's house, I made my way to the bathroom and stared at my reflection in the mirror. Under the harsh lights, I searched for some distinguishing mark. I leaned into the vanity and felt the line of the counter cut into my thighs. Nothing. Certainly, there had to be something left somewhere by everything I'd been through so people would know, but there was nothing except my normal, boring face. I couldn't shake this haunting feeling that the complexities of this second chance felt oddly similar to the complexities of my first.

February 21, 1984. [17 years old] I'm down on the scale, but I'm not really dieting. I guess you could call it binging and purging. I haven't really been doing it too smart. But no one is noticing that I'm thinner so...

March 21, 1984 [17 years old] I stopped throwing up for about two weeks...Then I headed to Mom's, where they were in the middle of a huge meal. So stupid me sat down and joined them. Then I proceeded to go upstairs to the only bathroom. Right as I finished Sandy came up and I just about shit. I cleaned off the toilet and started washing my face. She asked, "Did you just throw up?" "No," I answered. I was so nervous. I'm sure she knew. That was my first lie. I felt awful saying it, but I just couldn't admit it... The next morning Mom sat next to me on the bed and told me, while crying, that she had spent her last sleepless night over me.

When she finally reached the end of her words, she blew her nose, turned her face to the sky, and waited for me to say something, but I said nothing, so she shook her head and walked out. I sat motionless in the weight of her absence and then made my way down their creaky staircase and through their open kitchen past the farmhouse table. I walked the gravel road away from being misunderstood at Mom's.

I tried to slow my breathing, but my feet were moving as if I'd just been kicked in the side with a sharp spur. With a heavy foot, an open mouth, and no bra, I ran. The road turned and my lungs burned until I arrived out of breath and collapsed on my back at the fork in the road. *Without her, who am I? Without cancer or bulimia, who am I? Who am I?*

The Recovery

I moved to college in the fall to pursue a Bachelor of Arts in Communication with an emphasis in television production. Over the next four years, I slowly developed a sense of self outside of my body image by no longer pretending everything was okay. Instead, I acknowledged that there were lots of overwhelming times in a day and that I had to find a way to deal. I knew I had to eat, so I slid my tray along the buffet in the dining hall where I took small portions of food and tried to stay engaged in conversation instead of obsessing about where the nearest bathroom was. *Baby steps*, I told myself. *Little bites.*

December [Undated], 1987. [21 years old] I finished [another] semester. My classes ranged from Advanced Humanities Writing to Abnormal Psychology. I loved it. I feel like I say that after each semester—how lucky I am!

On the morning of my final long-term care appointment to monitor my Hodgkin's Disease at Children's Hospital, the sun rose just like it would on any other day, but the significance didn't escape me.

"Welcome back, Miss Terri," said my doctor, who still seemed to carry her broad shoulders with a strong back; her only sign of ageing was a thinning head of hair pulled into a sad ponytail.

As she looked at the chart, I panicked. *Had she just read some terrible results from my morning x-rays and blood work? What if the news is really bad? Am I up for a fight? Could I subject myself to chemotherapy, radiation, amputations and more because I'm hopeful? Because I want more time? Puh-lease!* I felt like such a hypocrite.

"Terri," she said, unruffled, "I am happy to tell you there are no new growths." She let the words come out slowly as if each were sent in their own fragile, iridescent bubble. I sat there with a stupid look on my face and imagined the buoyant bubbles floating around me against the light, their sensitive protective coating beautiful and vulnerable until they were nothing but a shower of mist. The little girl inside of me blinked back tears. "The question I have for you is, are you okay with being okay?"

"What's that supposed to mean?" I asked, feeling that indistinguishable rise in body temperature.

"What I'm asking is, can you take care of yourself?" I felt the tide erode from under my feet as if I were standing at a beckoning shoreline with my jeans rolled up, watching the sun go down while getting bitten by a swarm of sand fleas.

"You're a young woman with your whole life ahead of you."

I shot my hands up in a stop-in-the-name-of-love fashion. I did not need another get-back-in-the-game speech; I needed her to stop talking so I could have a moment to remind myself not to react badly. I knew I was a young woman with my whole life ahead of me, for Christ's sake. I'm not an idiot. I also knew what I needed to hear wasn't going to come from her. The truth needed to come from me.

I needed to make a choice: either I could continue harboring my secret, pretending to be fine, holding my life and feelings at bay, or I could tear down the labyrinth of associations I'd yanked and pulled and knotted together. During my long pause, I softened my fingers, lowered my arms, and realized that if I didn't make a move, away from the relentless fleas, I'd get eaten alive.

"I hear you," I said as I turned away from what I was ashamed to admit. "But," I went on, afraid if I stopped speaking my mouth would shut and I might never finish this sentence aloud, "I don't know how to do this."

"Sorry..."

"I don't know how to be a survivor."

"What do you mean?"

"I don't know how to be a survivor. My life with cancer was good. I mean, it wasn't good, it was easy. I mean, it wasn't easy, but it was easier than life." I started to pace the room. "After Mom left, I tried to figure out who I was without her, but," I stared up into the hot air balloon graphic over the fluorescent light on the ceiling and felt tears slide down my face and off my earlobe. "Can I take care of myself?" I laughed. "I never wished myself sick, you know? I wasn't suicidal or anything."

"Okay."

"I mean, maybe I was. Maybe, I was bulimic because I was too afraid of dealing with—my feelings. It made me feel better, but then I got really sick and I got to go on autopilot. I didn't have to deal with anything."

"Mmm Hmm," was all she could manage to add.

"I know, it's complicated, right? And then," I capitulated, feeling my resistance weakening. "Death came along in his smart suit and offered me this awesome finale, and I thought, hell yeah, I'm in. I totally trusted him, and I waited for him through all of those awful treatments. I waited for him to rescue me like Paula waited for Zack. He just never came back for me."

Doctor Crouse handed me a box of tissues with compassionate eyes as she wadded a few tissues in her hand in a show of support.

"I really thought dying was my purpose, that their memory of me was...was just going to freeze me heroically, you know? I just wanted to be remembered. I just wanted a shortcut through the pain of enduring more change. I wasn't a fighter. I didn't fight for anything much less to live with all the expectations attached to being a teen cancer survivor." I rolled my eyes and suddenly had to gasp for air, "I didn't fight for my life, and everyone thought I did." Then I began speaking again, this time slowly, in an impassioned tone, "And now? If I mention this to anyone, I look like a fraud. I try to make good life choices, but there's this relentless ambivalence and nagging skepticism plus the guilt of not feeling like a survivor, and I just can't. I'm not."

"Okay, Terri," she said in a soothing tone I'd never heard her use before. "That was a lot." We both laughed a little, which broke the tension as she knelt down awkwardly in front of me. "Listen, you didn't cause your cancer. You hear me?" I shrugged my shoulders and gave her a little smile from behind my wet tissue. "And, as far as what you think people expect from you, I mean, that's all so tricky because anybody who expects anything from you without discussing those expectations with you first is simply misguided."

"Ha."

"I know. I have parents, too," she said. "Here's where I think you're wrong."

"Oh, great," I laughed.

"I don't think you have to be a 5k-running survivor. Terri, how other people think your life should look is on them. Not your problem. Your problem is that you don't know what your life should look like or feel like and you need to find another way of handling all of it, a way that doesn't include destructive methods. I think you know you've got plenty of other ways to handle the tipping points of your life. When you're ready to start using all of those tools, you'll be off and running, handling life stuff like the rest of us."

"I never said anything about wanting to run."

"Hate to break it to you, kid, but we're all broken. Everybody comes with some emotional baggage. My mother once told me the secret to emotional baggage is to pack lightly or be willing to carry the load."

"Did you listen?"

"Well, my mother's a hoarder, so..."

Over the next decades, I dug in and used my diary to figure out what mattered and why but kept feeling the pull of my twelve-year-old self. She feared that if I ignored the foreboding part of myself I kept tethered like a balloon on a string around my wrist that the string would unwind and she would be forever lost. Not possible, I assured the worried little girl before taking her hand and moving on.

September [Undated], 1988. [22 years old] The weather is changing. Changing. East or West? She lingers, still unsure. She searches for an answer. So, friends, gather round [as] the memoirs of this womanhood continue.

I systematically checked items off my list as I loaded them into my luggage destined for New York City. Only after the case was shut did I notice the anxieties I had grown up with staring at me like gym class peers waiting to be chosen for a team. Instead of trying to pick the least disabling characteristic to be on my team, I opened the bag and invited them all to dive in and get comfortable alongside my joy, peace, and panties.

I woke up in Manhattan with a sense that my doctor was right. I was learning the hard way, which is sometimes the only way, that no matter how far I'd come or how perfect I wanted my life to look, the challenge of tipping points with food, family, self-confidence, and self-esteem would always be with me in varying degrees.

October [Undated], 1988. [22 years old] I got a phone call for an interview, that night I was hired.

November 19, 1988. [22 years old] Eureka! I got a promotion. From assistant to the executive producers to associate coordinating producer plus a $1,500 raise.

The eating disorder that had previously dictated my schedule would not just suddenly disappear but needed to be soothed for years. I didn't have time for it, but it still demanded my attention. I had to go to lunch with my co-workers and be able to participate in normal conversation. I sent my eyes all over the menu in search of something I could eat that wouldn't push me up, up, up to a tipping point while still participating in normal conversation. I felt like I was negotiating with the bully again, except this time I wasn't afraid to speak up.

January [Undated], 1989. [22 years old] ... unlike drugs or alcohol that are removed from a diet all together. A food addict must learn to take its worst enemy in small doses. Have you your own spot that gets you every time? Whether it be something you do to yourself (always go for the wrong type of person, collapse under the perils of peer pressure), something that just seems to always make you crazy? It makes me mad— so completely frustrated—that I am able to defeat myself and yet I will not—would not ever choose to have anyone or anything defeat me. Crazy. Really fucking crazy.

The longer I lived outside my web of illness and love, the better I was able to see another perspective of myself—as a person who wanted to embrace life and wasn't afraid to face change. By turning to the one constant relationship in my life—writing— I found the words to express the doubt that I could handle it and welcomed the cathartic purge like a child collapsing into a pile of autumn leaves.

February [Undated], 1990. [23 years old] I've got to re-gather my nutrition shit back together. The path I've chosen is not the one I want to stay on, "wrong road" she screamed. This is not working for me and because the only person who can change anything is me then I better fucking do it. I just better do it. I better. A refrigerator is not a meal and cranberry juice and vodka is not a substitute. What is it? What is it that is so rewarding that I can't give it up?

I turned to my diary like it was my best friend or therapist without knowing that by listening to my conscience I was not only writing my life, but creating an awareness that I was having a life...or that asking myself—and answering—hard questions was a psychological release. I just needed to talk to somebody I could trust. My diaries are authentic and my story is true, but my struggle to develop a sense of a self worth fighting for is universal.

PS: 14 Years Later

June 18, 2004. [37 years old] I kissed Mom and [her new partner] Pat before climbing the stairs for bed but didn't go to sleep right away. I lay there knowing that being here at my mother's house was no mistake. I am a woman looking for a girl who was looking for herself.

In June of 2004, I am in Buffalo Creek to convalesce with Mom and Pat. I have just ended a marriage, moved home from Los Angeles, and am looking for work as a freelance television producer when I find myself listening from the hallway as Mom puts my sweaty and exhausted seven year-old-son down for a nap with a quirky commentary on how any type of pie could solve world problems. I smile as I listen from the hallway and let the smell of her Halston unravel me.

Ever since I arrived home and pulled the vintage suitcases full of my life's diaries from storage, Mom and I have been screaming at each other. She's convinced I'm the spirited teenage cancer survivor. And while it's true that cancer played an important role in my bewilderment about my identity and direction, to present myself only as a survivor would be a lie. Mom also thinks the eating disorder came after cancer; she does not know it started when she left. *How can I explain to her how deeply affected I was by everything that happened between us without sounding like a daughter blaming her mother?*

We are just now taking seats opposite each other outside on her porch to hash it out. We have no idea how long this will take or what painful truths it might reveal, but we both know our relationship is worth the struggle.

"All we heard after the bad news [the diagnosis] was good news—the cancer could be cured. It's why your diaries are so important—you are finally getting back in touch with the 16-year-old Terri and seeing that you were not devastated by the news of your disease but merely challenged. Maybe the message in all of this...the benefit of your experience to others could be that one must not necessarily be miserable to be creative. My dear girl, perhaps it is enough to have known misery."

"Mom, stop. You can't edit my experience. I can't let you do that anymore, just stand there and tell me how I should feel about the divorce and cancer and what I should or shouldn't write about. I have my own feelings about how everything went down, and I need you to just let me...just let me have them, please." I've surprised us both by finding the nerve and the voice to speak to my mother this way.

"I can't tell you where your illness came from or why," she squints at me and continues. "You weren't bleeding anywhere," Mom says with a clenched fist and a firm pointer finger, "and you certainly weren't telling anyone that you were hurting."

I chew on my lip and then agree. "You're right."

"How was anyone supposed to know?"

"You're totally right."

"How was I supposed to know?"

"I didn't know."

"What's that supposed to mean?"

"I didn't know I was hurting, Mom."

"I hope you have a purpose when writing about all this hurt and pain you were inflicting on yourself and making some sense of why you were doing whatever you were doing and that you have something to share with your readers that will make someone's life better."

"Mom, you're doing it again."

"What?"

"Telling me how to feel."

"Are you trying to connect disease to divorce? Who exactly are you blaming for your choice to self-harm? Who will benefit from your experience?"

"Who will benefit? What about me, Mom? Aren't I worth it?"

"Of course..."

"You're talking about cancer and you leaving, but you're not talking about me."

"Listen, Terri. You are an outstanding writer and person, but be real careful about being stuck in victim mode without a purpose, or it really will make you sick."

Suddenly, my curly-haired boy appears in the doorway and then on my lap where he leans his warm body against me; I wrap my arms around him, lean over, and kiss the pillow crease on his cheek.

"Hi," I whisper.

He pulls away for a moment and asks, "We still going to the pot roast?"

"What?" I look at Mom with a quizzical look.

"Are we still going?"

"To the pot roast?" I laugh. "Oh, you mean the potluck? Yes, yep. We're still going."

"Do you need a dish?" Mom asks as we all break from our places. "We've got loads of chicken from the grill, don't we, Pat?"

"No, thanks. It's a dessert thing," I explain as I stand, signaling the end. "We should go."

Mom and Pat's two Golden Retrievers bookend Sam as he walks to our car. Mom and I walk the driveway behind them, suddenly under a normalcy spell.

"Bye, Grammy. Bye, Pat," Sam says as he climbs into the back of our Camry.

"Scoot your bum back, please." I ask in an English accent as I lean over him to clip his booster seat belt and then give him a kiss before leaning back out of the car.

"You may write," Mom explains as my back presses into my driver's side door, "about how I left you and how you had to suffer alone with life after cancer." We stare at each other. "But, the self-pain," her voice changes to a whisper, "I could never do that to me. I love me too much."

I clench my mouth and lift my brows.

"Are you still doing that?" she asks.

"No."

"Not at all?"

"No."

"Good. That's good." Mom bows her head against mine. "Because you are a survivor, Terri." She wraps her arms around me and rocks slowly back and forth. "Even if it's a reluctant one."

"I know, Ma." I tell her as I pull the door between us.

"Love you, my Terri."

"Love you, too, Ma."

With my arm hanging out the window, and my fingers lazily waving goodbye, I drive away. Truth is, I'm not purging anymore, but that doesn't mean I don't find myself ascending in a clickity-clackity coaster cart next to my feeble foreboding bully self again and again. What I do know is that, like the scores of other addicts who find the will to make better choices every day, I do, too. Good for them. Good for me.

As a serial autobiographer Terri has filled 46 diaries since she was ten years old. Terri and her mother can be heard discussing their story on The Mortified Podcast, a proud member of Radiotopia, from PRX. The podcast transitions to their story beginning at 12:15 https://beta.prx.org/stories/277515. Terri doesn't tweet or facebook or post pics of flowers and cats or follow anybody or want to be followed by anybody, but she does dial up now and again to use the worldwide interweb :) and can be reached at terriporter1@gmail.com.

Improving Chances for a Healthy Recovery

Recovering from an eating disorder is difficult. It takes hard work, consultation with a team of professionals, and support from friends and loved ones.

Just as no eating disorder is exactly the same, recovery can look different for different people. The length of time and intensity of the recovery process can vary for each person depending on the severity and duration of their eating disorder and the presence of other mental health concerns.

"There are many factors I consider when assessing how someone might progress toward and into recovery from an eating disorder," says Deanna Linville, Ph.D., LMFT, Associate Professor of Marriage and Family Therapy at the University of Oregon and eating disorder specialist. Those factors include the following:

- **The length of time someone has suffered.** The shorter the eating disorder, the better chance of full recovery, but people whose eating disorders have lasted for longer are still able to experience full recovery.
- **Severity of symptoms.** The more severe the symptoms, the more difficult the recovery, but recovery is still possible.
- **Strength and resources of the sufferer.** Examples include the sufferer's motivation for recovery, commitment to recovery, and willingness to be helped.
- **External and internal reinforcers of the eating disorder and recovery.** Sustained recovery will be more difficult if the sufferer continues to live in an environment that reinforces the eating disorder or the secondary gains of the eating disorder, e.g. the person only receives love and care during mealtimes.

- **Severity and source of body image disturbance and dissatisfaction.** The amount of time recovery takes can depend on what has caused body image issues and the length of time body image disturbance has been present. For instance, a patient who has heard criticism of their body repeatedly for decades may take longer to work through those issues.
- **Emotional dis-regulation or regulation.** Studies have shown that people with eating disorders tend to have a more difficult time regulating and congruently expressing their emotions, e.g. controlling their behaviors when struggling with difficult emotions or using strategies to change their emotional responses. Sufferers who are able to develop these emotional regulation strategies typically achieve more success in recovery.
- **Severity and ability to treat comorbid conditions, such as obsessive compulsive disorder, depression, PTSD, and substance use disorders.** Recovery can take longer when there are additional mental health concerns to work through.
- **Attempted solutions.** What has the person already tried? To what extent did that solution work and why?

According to Linville and other eating disorder experts, it is possible for a person suffering from an eating disorder to improve their chances of recovery. The chances of experiencing a healthy recovery improve when those affected by eating disorders have hope. "I like to encourage my clients to think about their values, what really matters to them, and who they could be without the eating disorder," says Linville.

The following can facilitate a health recovery:

- **Social supports that are in place or can be cultivated.** Numerous studies have highlighted the importance of social support for healthy recovery. In a study published in the journal *Eating Disorders*, for instance, Linville and colleague Tiffany Brown, Senior Lecturer and Clinical Director in the Couples and Family Therapy graduate program at the University of Oregon, report the following: "Based on the data from the current study, eating disorder recovery is influenced by the individual's connection to self and others, their relationships, and the focus of care. Participants reported needing reconnection, both internally and externally, and explained that these connections played a role in their overall recovery experience."
- **Motivation and hope for recovery.** What's important here is not just that the sufferer wants to get better but their motivation and whether they believe they can be successful. It can be helpful to encourage those suffering to externalize their eating disorder from who they are as a person. An eating disorder can be a part of one's identity but not encapsulate all that the person is even while they are immersed in suffering.
- **Ability of care system to mobilize and join with the individual (not the eating disorder) toward improving their health.** This can be achieved by helping social supports understand what an eating disorder is. Their role in supporting a person toward recovery is often a necessary ingredient to sustained recovery. (See "Families and Eating Disorder Recovery")
- **Access to quality care.** Quality care can take many different forms, including therapy focused on eating disorder recovery. It is typically recommended that people seeking recovery from eating disorders be cared for by a multidisciplinary team, including an individual

and family counselor/mental health provider; dietitian; and/or primary care physician.

Recovering from an eating disorder is possible, as the essays in this book demonstrate, and there are many different pathways to recovery. Working toward putting into place the resources listed above can increase the likelihood of a successful outcome.

My eating disorder was one of the most difficult things in my life, but as in the book of Job, God used my struggle and turned it around to give me a hope-filled future.

—Mark

My Personal Exodus – One Man's Story

Mark

Even in grade school I remember feeling unsure of myself and my place in the world.

I was raised in a good Catholic home and had everything I needed, but for some reason I was starving for approval and acceptance. So, I'd achieve straight A's, win the talent show, and do other things to earn praise from others.

But starting in middle school I was faced with the reality that I couldn't achieve the same grades. I was also emotionally unprepared for being "unpopular" and excluded from social circles.

High school was more of the same. I drifted through my teen years, as my parents were super busy working to support us, and my popular, soccer star brother moved away to college. So, I pursued a new way to seek affirmation and attention as the lead guitarist and singer for a number of local bands.

That quickly opened the door to two very addicting things in my life: alcohol and a number of serious, long-term relationships with girlfriends. I lived alone for most of college, and both of those distractions provided escape from the pain of my insecurity. But by the time I was 21, I was done with destructive drinking. I had become disillusioned by the politics of trying to make it in the music industry. And, the sense of abandonment after each failed relationship was emotionally devastating.

During my junior year of college, I decided I would work at the beach in Nags Head, North Carolina during the summer. That's when my desperate quest for identity transformed into an eating disorder. The thought was, *If I get in shape, work out, and get six-pack abs before the summer, I will meet another young woman and life will be great again.* I got in shape (including the abs) but when my plan didn't work, I just kept on with the extreme dieting and exercise regimen because I didn't know what else to do.

As my senior year drew to a close, I was completely alone and directionless. My goal of getting in shape had transformed into an unhealthy monster that now controlled me, and I was tired of being my own worst enemy. So, I sought counseling and participated in group therapy, but the addiction and bondage continued to consume my entire life. Within a month after graduating college, I was inpatient at a mental hospital, severely depressed, and at risk of death from what I had done to my body.

Around that time, I remember visiting my parent's priest for encouragement and direction. As I was walking through the parking lot of the church, a curious question popped into my mind. *What if everything you learned about Me in church as a child, like Noah's Ark, was actually true?* I really didn't know where the thought came from or if God was somehow speaking to my heart, so I prayed a simple prayer, "God if you are real, and you really do care about me, then I need you to save me from this because I'm not going to make it on my own. I am going to die." His relentless, loving intervention after that prayer was amazing and still humbles me today.

I prefer to call my recovery process "my personal exodus." If you're not familiar with the term "exodus," it's about God delivering the Israelites from cruel oppression in Egypt. When they tried to escape the pursuing Egyptian army, they faced certain doom when they were blocked by the Red Sea. Then God parted the sea and made a miraculous way of escape. That's <u>exactly</u> what God did for me. The eating disorder was my cruel oppressor and enemy. My best attempts to recover were like me trying to part the Red Sea. I needed Him to make the way of escape for me.

After that parking lot prayer, I remember discovering a radio station I had never heard before. The lyrics of the songs really gave me hope. It was no accident I landed on that radio station. I later learned the lyrics were Scripture verses in a song by a Christian music artist. I kept listening, and despite feeling a little awkward, I went to a Christian bookstore and bought a Bible for more encouragement. I started reading the Book of Job, about a man who suffered and lost everything and then was restored by God. For the first time, I read the Gospels about Jesus and was deeply moved.

The head nurse of my support group was an encouraging Christian woman, an eating disorder survivor herself. I was offered a job where a Christian coworker and her fiancé kept reaching out to me, caring for me, and inviting me over for dinner. I met a Christian businessman and youth pastor who asked me to come live with them. And I was invited to a Baptist church Superbowl party where I was accepted by everyone despite my appearance and social quirks. God blessed me with friends who liked me for who I was, not my performance or status. And trust me, joining that Baptist church, with so many picnics and potluck meals, gave me plenty of opportunities to begin overcoming my anxiety of eating with others.

I became fully aware of all the ways God was answering that simple parking lot prayer. He had encouraged me with the Bible, given me caring friends, provided for me financially, given me a new home with mentors, and invited me into a loving Christian community.

Then at the end of that Easter's church service, the pastor extended an invitation for people to hand over the control of their life to Jesus Christ. Then he repeated the invitation multiple times, which was unusual. I had heard the invitation almost every week, but this time it felt different, deeply personal, urgent. I can best describe it as God speaking to my heart and mind like in a direct message. He wanted me to exchange all those years of drifting and destructive self-reliance for His forgiveness and a life of freedom for His good purposes. And I did ask Jesus to become the Lord of who I was and where my life was going. It was an emotional decision but also an informed one after reading and believing the claims of the Bible for myself.

When I made that decision, it wasn't an immediate, miraculous end to the eating disorder. I still had some hang-ups with food and exercise. But God gave me balance and accountability to work through those one step at a time, one victory at a time. I met a better counselor who allowed me to incorporate my faith into our sessions. I was shocked the day she said I didn't need ongoing counseling but to call her if I needed to. She was another gift from God who equipped me to move forward. I was able to carefully wean off of antidepressant and anti-anxiety meds, which had been a necessary part of my treatment. I'd say my eating returned to normal after a few months.

That freedom enabled me to become a missionary traveling to schools around the United States. Soon afterwards I met my wife, who was unlike any woman I'd ever met, grounded in her identity in Jesus.

I returned to music, writing and recording a couple of personal songs about the healing process. God opened doors for me to do concerts in churches, schools, colleges, coffeehouses, a summer camp, even an amusement park. It was a privilege to share my hopeful story with so many people impacted by an eating disorder.

It's been quite a few years since all this happened. And I'll admit knowing God doesn't eliminate all of life's problems. In fact, Jesus promises we'll have trouble on this side of Heaven. Life can be hard. But I can honestly say I don't worry about food any more, something that used to consume just about every thought I once had. From time to time I still do have thoughts of insecurity or the temptation to control things I can't. I think we all do to some degree or another.

So, every day I like to check in with God and strengthen that relationship. I open my Bible to read about Him and thank Him for rescuing me and for His good plans for my life. I also have a good deal of accountability in my life, with my wife, my Christian male friends, and our small group from church. If big challenges come up, our family also has a trusted Christian counselor we can see. The healthiest people I know get counseling when life gets rough. All these things help me have God's perspective instead of relying on my own determination, which can still get me into trouble.

My eating disorder was one of the most difficult things in my life, but as in the book of Job, God used my struggle and turned it around to give me a hope-filled future. You might be in the midst of struggling with an eating disorder right now and can't even imagine a way of escape. If so, I trust you will be encouraged by this invitation from Jesus recorded in Matthew 11:28-30:

"Come to me, all you who are weary and burdened, and I will give you rest. Take my yoke upon you and learn from me, for I am gentle and humble in heart, and you will find rest for your souls. For my yoke is easy and my burden is light."

Mark is a graduate of the VCU School of the Arts. He is co-owner and creative director of a Midwest branding agency as well as a professional photographer. He's most thankful for his wonderful wife and son and enjoys traveling with them any chance he can.

The last revelation that kick-started continued healing was that my distorted image of my body just isn't enough to stop me from eating or living life to its fullest.

—Nina Ward

Living Life to the Fullest

by Nina Ward

I will always see myself as fat, and that's just the way it is. But I will never starve myself to near death again.

In February 1983, when I was in my late 20s, friends and family sent me newspaper and magazine clippings about the death of the popular singer Karen Carpenter. The cause of death was heart failure resulting from anorexia nervosa. Karen Carpenter's death had brought awareness to an illness not often talked of before then. News articles appeared with frightful information on what happens when a body goes without food. People tried endlessly to warn me that I was heading down the same path.

Three weeks later, I lay void of energy, motionless on the couch while my three young children played. I could barely breathe. I had hit rock bottom.

After years of digesting next to nothing, my symptoms had grown worse. Family and friends made fun of my weight and irregular eating habits, although I couldn't understand why. My stomach had shrunk along with any common sense; my brain was malfunctioning.

What seemed like normal eating habits to me were obviously not normal to others. How I saw my body shape was not the same as how others saw it.

By this time, my menstrual cycle rarely appeared, and my energy level was about to hit zero. My cognitive function was impaired from not consuming enough food. I hated that I couldn't focus. I loathed being lethargic. I missed the hyper-spastic person I was when I had as much energy as a two-year-old and a Jack Russell Terrier puppy combined. When I suffered from an eating disorder, no one would ever have believed there was a time when people had nicknamed me the energizer bunny!

Maybe I would have continued down that path if it weren't for Carpenter's death. Her passing brought light. After learning about Carpenter's death, I realized my own eating disorder was way out of hand. It was as if my eyes were struggling to see through eyeglasses covered in mud until someone wiped and washed them off until I could see clearly. Carpenter's death saved my life.

The Turning Point

That day I lay on the couch, the baby screamed in his swing in front of me. I desperately tried to raise my left arm to give the swing a push, but my hand only fell to the carpet. My husband had recently abandoned the family, and a bit of depression had seeped into my life with a ton of overwhelming concerns. The fact that I couldn't even move to take care of my infant son hit me like slabs of stone. I questioned if I was dying. According to the anorexia research I'd done, organ failure was possible. This was my first scare.

My voice, barely a whisper, instructed my seven-year-old son to get a neighbor. When two neighbor friends found me listless on the couch, I listened to their scolding, ready to accept help. My friends boldly explained I had two choices: Lose my kids and possibly die or get to a doctor and live. Those facts washed over me like cold water hitting a sleeping face. I finally awakened to the hard truth: I was struggling with anorexia.

The neighbors phoned another neighbor to watch the kids while we went to the hospital. By now things had become almost dire. My muscle tissue was being eaten away. My immune system was lowering. The fear of being overweight ate at my body and mind like turpentine on paint.

The hospital stay wasn't long, but the incident shot enough fear in me to wake me up. The Department of Social Services would take my kids away if I didn't get help. This time I was ready. The thought of losing my kids tore my heart out even more than the fear of death. I decided I needed to live for ny kids.

What kind of mother allows herself to be controlled by this kind of illness? Thoughts of incompetence raced through my mind. These thoughts were the first round of ammunition in the recovery battle. Like bullets knocking out the bad guys, they propelled me to get well one day at a time.

I believe my eating disorder was not about body image alone; food just never interested me. My mother used to say she would feed me portions of what so-called normal babies ate, and I'd spit it out. When I was an infant, my parents often had to nudge me awake for feedings. Physicians label babies with this behavior as lazy eaters. Becoming a *foodie* was never my destiny.

Perhaps I didn't eat because I didn't want to become obese like my mom. She stood only five feet tall and carried so much weight she could barely move. I'd seen how her weight had developed into a disability for her, placing limits on her life and robbing her of joy. She never learned to drive because she feared getting stuck between the seat and the steering wheel! She was conscious of things like sinking a boat and waited at home each time my dad took me boating. She was ashamed of her limitations and appearance. Just like my own food thoughts, her weight consumed her daily. As a child, I remember both of us standing in front of the fridge crying. She wanted to stop bingeing. I needed to start eating. Fear of following in my mom's footsteps to obesity can be a part of my subconscious thinking even to this day.

After the hospital adventure, I took a thorough, close-up look at myself, without realizing I was taking the first of many steps towards recovery. Gradually I learned that food was essential to life whether I was hungry or not.

Besides a myriad of prayers and support from family and friends, using the Alcohol Anonymous Program's steps with which I was already familiar played a key part in my success story. It worked for me once upon a time, so why not live by that *one day at a time* motto again?

Retraining my brain was the first big step towards eating disorder recovery. Because the brain is a muscle and depriving your brain of food causes malfunctions, this was a colossal mandatory step that took months.

Four of my friends took shifts for five weeks, making sure I received enough nutrition to survive and regain the ability to consume foods. I practiced eating soft foods, bringing the spoon to my mouth and swallowing a few bites at a time, gradually increasing the amounts. I groaned at anything I had to cut or chew. It just seemed like too much work. For many years after recovery, my boyfriends would cut my meat just so I would eat some protein!

Each year, anorexia recedes further from my world. It no longer defines me. I got to this point with self-help strategies and lots of prayers. I have always analyzed everything into another orbit, over-planned, and set enough goals for two lifetimes. These traits equipped me with the tools needed for the situation and gave me a good kick-ass start.

Putting myself on a regular eating schedule made it easier to acclimate to a new daily routine. During the day, when the kids were away at school, I used a clock timer with a loud ring to cue me when mealtime approached. I'd then drop whatever I was doing to prepare a meal. Eventually, that ritual wasn't needed anymore. As you might be able to tell, I unknowingly kept things very scientific and non-emotional.

At first, I mentally prepared my mind to force food into my mouth and swallow until it became a habit. Just like any habit, learned behavior changes the neurological patterns and becomes automatic. It was all about patience. Over time things did become much easier.

One of the other strategies I learned was to listen to my body. I'm not sure where this revelation came from. I had tuned my body out for so many long years that I was not familiar with it anymore. Ignoring hunger pains at the beginning of the anorexic journey escalated to the point where I soon felt nothing. Neglect caused me to disconnect with not only my outward appearance but my insides as well. Similar to a relationship of any kind, if you don't listen to someone, you can't know who he or she truly is. If you don't spend time with someone, there is no relationship.

For a few years, it became a battle to consume enough to sustain a healthy life. At least I was out of the danger zone. Yet, at times, I would still stand in front of the fridge in tears trying to think of something I could consume.

Eating issues followed me from childhood to adulthood, so I became used to preparing a protocol for better health. My parents had tried all kinds of tricks, bribes, and plans to entice me to eat. What helps me the most, to this day, is planning the day's menu the day before or first thing in the morning. If I don't, I tend to ignore hunger pangs, or I don't eat enough calories or protein for the day.

To crave or enjoy a favorite food was beyond my comprehension until a new chapter in my life began. Since I'd never been sick a day in my life, except on a rare occasion with the flu, it was a shock to discover breast cancer at the age of forty-three. Cancer is hard, but it has its perks, including brand new soft hair! Another perk for me was the ability to crave a food and delight in a meal.

When I was receiving chemotherapy treatments, there were specific foods I craved. That food became the only nourishment I could stomach for weeks. I was able to imagine a grilled cheese sandwich or a milkshake nourishing my body, confident it would soothe my newfound hunger and give me what I needed to fight the cancer beast.

Everyone remarked how good I looked with the weight gain during treatments! I might have been bald, jaundiced, and lifeless, but I sure looked good with a little meat on my bones! My mom nearly fell off the chair when I finished off a sandwich and chips! That was something she had never seen before. My portions increased even more.

Today, I still look at myself and see fat. That's okay. I know in my head that I am not. I know my eyes are deceiving me. In fact, I often praise myself on my decent figure, especially for my age. I also am one hundred percent sure it is impossible that I could ever be overweight. It's not in my nature. My lifestyle doesn't lead down that road. It's not in my life plan, a plan I now have control over.

The last revelation that kick-started continued healing was that my distorted image of my body just isn't enough to stop me from eating or living life to its fullest, no pun intended!

Nina Ward is a published author of nonfiction and fiction for adults' and children's publications and a retired massage therapist. Nina is a born New York City girl but has had the opportunity to reside in various states across the United States. When she is not writing, you can find her kayaking along a lazy river or embracing a beach sunset, enjoying God's gifts.

The more I accepted myself, the less shame I felt, and the less shame I felt, the less room there seemed to be for my eating disorder.

—Megan Campbell

Finding Light through Darkness

Megan Campbell

As a child of divorced parents, I often felt unseen, unheard, and misunderstood by my split family. It was exhausting to go back and forth between my parent's houses while dealing with the emotional difficulties they each faced. A part of me felt personally responsible for my parents' unhappiness, and I constantly struggled to gain my balance without knowing where middle ground was.

I don't blame my parents for my eating disorder, but the events that took place in my childhood and adolescence served as a perfect storm. Pain, shame, disappointment, and misunderstandings built inside me early on, and because I didn't have the skillset to express those deep and intense emotions—or anyone to express them to—my eating disorder became my outlet, my escape.

While riding the emotional rollercoaster of my parent's divorce, I also struggled to accept that I was gay. In high school, I realized I was different from most of my friends. I was never boy crazy; I didn't have much interest in boys at all. Instead, I would idolize girls in a way that I felt wasn't "normal." As I got older, I began to put the puzzle pieces together and did everything in my power to try to change that part of myself. The shame surrounding that fact of my identity overpowered everything. It felt like starving myself could save me from having to face the terrifying truth I was trying so hard to deny.

For a long time, darkness swallowed me up. I struggled with depression, extremely low self-esteem and confidence, shame, self-hate, insecurity, lack of motivation, crippling shyness, and fear. All of those factors fed each other while they eventually starved me.

My eating disorder entirely removed me from reality and kept me in complete isolation. It was the one factor in my life I thought I could control and rely on when everything else felt out of control and unreliable. I became a servant to strict and rigid rules regarding food. The rules consumed every single thought I had, and the more I obeyed, the stronger the eating disorder seemed to become.

As my eating disorder continued to spiral out of control, it became a form of self-punishment. I felt that, because I had never experienced emotional fullness or satisfaction, I deserved to starve quite literally. There was something about the deprivation that felt intoxicating to me. It was a goal I could accomplish and something I finally felt good at.

Sadly enough, the more weight I lost before looking completely malnourished and significantly underweight, the more attention I got from peers. The compliments people gave me felt incredibly satisfying. For so long I had felt alone and invisible, so it was especially nice to have people notice me and give me attention. I was obsessed with the idea of being small and would thrive off of comments like, "You're so cute and little!" or "You're tiny!" In a sense, I felt like I finally had something other people envied. I had always compared myself to others and never felt good enough or pretty enough in most cases, but I finally had something others wanted.

At the same time, shrinking myself was a subconscious way for me to remain childlike. Since many of my needs were unmet when I was a child, a big part of me wasn't ready to enter adulthood and accept the fact that those needs might never be met.

As the years went by, my eating disorder got stronger while I became weaker. Every day felt like an exhausting battle. Physically, I was either in constant pain, lightheaded and weak, or shivering from cold. I could no longer focus in school because nothing could hold my attention longer than a few minutes; I was constantly immersed in a fog of starvation. My grades began to suffer, and I had completely stopped caring. I truly felt like I was just floating through life day after day, only existing and not truly living.

There were times when I would get into bed at night with extreme exhaustion, my body aching from constant hunger and deprivation. I would lie there and wonder if my body would decide to shut down while I was asleep.

The night before I started therapy, I was scared to even close my eyes because I realized I didn't want to die. Even though there had been plenty of moments when I had thought death might be the answer, that night I wasn't ready to die. I had this unexplainable feeling that I wasn't done on this earth quite yet. I knew my life had more meaning waiting on the other side. I just had to get there, but I had no idea how. All I knew was that I could not do it alone.

When I met my therapist and started taking steps towards recovery, I instantly felt like I would make it through. I finally felt seen and heard in a way I had never experienced before, and that feeling took power away from my eating disorder. For the first time, I felt like my feelings, emotions, and experiences were validated. Slowly but surely, the more I learned how to express myself, the less I felt the need to numb myself. In fact, I didn't want to feel numb anymore.

I began to find my voice again, and I learned that my true voice and the voice of my eating disorder were separate. I learned that I could actually talk back to my eating disorder by recognizing disordered thoughts.

It helped to imagine talking to myself in a way I would talk to a child or a close friend. I knew my eating disorder voice told me things I could not imagine saying to another person, let alone a child. That helped me recognize the two voices, and over time I learned how to have self-compassion. At first, it felt inauthentic, but the more I practiced accepting myself, the better I became at quieting the eating disorder voice. When that voice was loud, I would do the opposite of what it said. For example, if my eating disorder voice told me not to eat something, I would eat the exact thing it was telling me not to eat.

During that time I realized my eating disorder doesn't define me. I learned how to bridge the gap between my relationship with food, my relationship with myself, and my relationship with other people. Feeling my emotions for the first time in a very long time was admittedly terrifying. Often, it felt like a volcano had erupted inside of me; a flood of emotions would pour out. It took a long time to learn how to cry again because for years I hadn't let myself cry; I had used my eating disorder to numb my emotions. Once I finally allowed myself to cry, there were many moments when I would just start crying for no reason other than that my body had so much emotion it needed to release. The more I let go of those tears, the better I felt.

Working intensively with a therapist and dietician helped keep me on track, especially during the first few months of recovery when I was still unsure. I felt supported and knew I had people who believed in me, which ultimately helped me believe in myself. I was at a point where I had completely forgotten how to eat "normally," and my hunger and full cues felt nonexistent. I struggled greatly with body dysmorphia during this period in my recovery. It was exhausting at times, but learning about nutrition helped me view food and nourishment from an entirely different perspective. I put all of my trust into my treatment team, fully surrendering and focusing my energy on recovery and building a new life.

For most of my early life, I fought against who I was. When I began to turn towards my emotions, I opened up to the idea of getting to know myself. I remember feeling like I had been reborn. All of a sudden I was actually living my life and not just existing. The more I accepted myself, the less shame I felt, and the less shame I felt, the less room there seemed to be for my eating disorder. My real identity began to emerge.

I still have eating disorder thoughts at times, but when I do, I turn inward and ask myself what I am feeling and why. I try to understand my emotions with self-compassion. I used to be terrified of having these kinds of thoughts in recovery because I thought I was doing something wrong or that I wasn't strong enough to fully recover. Now, in a way, I am thankful for those thoughts because they usually pop up when there is something off balance; they remind me to process my emotions.

My eating disorder in a very strange way saved my life. It forced me to confront the emotional turmoil that had been developing inside of me and led me to find middle ground; it led me to light. I realize now that I was supposed to go through this, that the struggles happened to me for a reason. I finally accept myself and my story.

A year into my recovery, my therapist at the time asked me to write a thank you letter to my eating disorder. This is what I wrote:

Dear eating disorder,

Thank you for protecting me by keeping me numb from all of the pain in my life. You really did stop all of the hurt by numbing it. You protected me by keeping me all to yourself and kept me isolated for years so I wouldn't get hurt by other people. You kept me hidden in the dark so no one could see me. That was your way of protecting me. My life felt so completely out of control at the time, so you gave me a false sense of control that I thought I so desperately needed.

I realize now, however, that eventually you would have killed me. Without you, though, I would not be the person I am today. You drug me all the way down to rock bottom. You showed me what it was like to be on the brink of death. You showed me what it felt like to be in unbearable pain. You pulled me down so far, but then a miracle happened: you let me go, but instead of falling, I flew.

My recovery has been the most difficult and life-changing experience that has ever happened to me. I believe you made me so sick so that I would seek recovery. That is where I found strength. That is where I found myself.

I used to be ashamed of my eating disorder and the judgments of others. I now view my eating disorder as incredibly empowering. Going through it not only led me to who I am, it led me to find my passion. I realized through my recovery what nourishes and feeds my soul: helping others. I hope to eventually become a licensed marriage and family therapist. I have found my place in the world, and I hope that my fight will someday encourage someone else's. Recovery is possible.

Megan Campbell is soon to be starting her first year in Marriage, Couple, and Family Therapy in a Master's program with a plan to specialize in eating disorders. She hopes to become a licensed marriage, couple, and family therapist and pursue a doctoral degree so she can eventually work in academia as a researcher and clinical professor. Megan hopes to combine research, clinical work, and teaching to make the most impact.

The Role of Genetics and Environment in the Development of Eating Disorders

People choose to suffer from eating disorders, right? No. This pervasive myth can be damaging because it can affect the way therapists, family members, and others deal with sufferers. Eating disorders are a form of mental illness, and many experts believe a person does not choose to have an eating disorder any more than a person chooses to have schizophrenia.

Another pervasive myth? Society—particularly the media—causes eating disorders. There is an element of truth in that repeated exposure to images of "perfect" bodies can trigger behaviors that lead to eating disorders, but society does not cause eating disorders.

Truth: There is a genetic component to eating disorders.

"Research over the last several decades (primarily conducted with twins) has consistently shown that eating disorders **do** run in families," says Suzanne Mazzeo, Ph.D, Professor and Director of the Counseling Psychology Program at Virginia Commonwealth University. "Specifically, relatives of individuals with eating disorders are at 7-12 times higher risk of developing these disorders themselves."

Although eating disorders are as heritable as bipolar disorder and schizophrenia, there is less awareness of the genetic factors leading to eating disorders. "This lack of awareness can lead to misconceptions that affected individuals 'choose' to have these conditions, or can just 'snap out if it' and quit their problematic 'diets' if they really wanted to," says Mazzeo. "But this isn't true, and it isn't how we generally think about people with other medical conditions (e.g., diabetes or arthritis)."

Truth: Environment does play a role in the development of eating disorders.

Studies of eating disorder risk factors have revealed that, in addition to genetic factors, elements of our environment do play a role in eating disorder risk. "Scientists who conduct research with twins to elucidate both genetic and environmental risks for eating disorders divide the environment into that which is shared between twins (e.g., their family) and that which is unique (e.g., experiences/settings not shared with a co-twin)," says Mazzeo. Environmental factors unique to one twin could include participating in a sports team, experiencing trauma, or being bullied.

"The interplay of these various genetic and environmental factors sets the stage for eating disorders," says Mazzeo. When discussing the development of eating disorders, Cynthia Bulik, Distinguished Professor of Eating Disorders at the University of North Carolina, explains, "genes load the gun and environment pulls the trigger." The environment can either mitigate or exacerbate underlying genetic vulnerabilities. For example, participation in sports or other activities with an appearance or weight focus (e.g., gymnastics, ballet, modeling) can increase risk. "This doesn't necessarily mean that someone with a genetic risk shouldn't participate in those activities," says Mazzeo. "Families need to be aware, however, of 'red flags' in both the environment of that activity and in their children's behaviors and attitudes while participating." Also, weight or appearance-related teasing can be particularly problematic for someone whose genetics lead to an increased susceptibility to an eating disorder.

How to decrease the risk of developing eating disorders:

Because there are both genetic and environmental components to eating disorders, parents wonder if it is possible to prevent the development of eating disorders. Many experts say people can decrease the level of risk. "It's essential to remember that your genes are not your destiny!" says Mazzeo. "Many strategies can be used to reduce eating disorder risk in all types of families."

Here are some strategies for minimizing risk:

- **Model healthy eating.** "This means teaching (in an age-appropriate manner) the value of nutrition and emphasizing the value of eating well for health, vs. appearance-related reasons," says Mazzeo. It is also important to consider how we talk about foods. We aren't "good" or "bad" because of how we ate; a day is not "good" or "bad" because of our dietary choices. "Rather than describing a food as 'good' or 'bad,'" says Mazzeo, "consider talking openly about how you feel after eating it."
- **Be aware of your children's "unique environment."** What are their friends, coaches, and other important people around them saying about appearance, healthy eating, and exercise? If you have concerns about a coach's attitude regarding weight or appearance, talk with him or her, and, if need be, change teams. There are many sports and even performance options that accept various body sizes and types. "Teach your child about weight stigma," says Mazzeo, "and talk openly about why this stigma has such negative effects on others."

- **Develop media literacy.** Help your child understand that images are often manipulated. There are many online resources that show how photo editing completely transforms images of individuals to make them fit an "ideal" that is rarely (if ever) found in the real world.
- **Discuss genetic risks for eating disorders, just as you would discuss breast cancer genes.** "Being aware of risk can empower you to do something about it," says Mazzeo.
- **For all families, but especially those with a genetic risk, be aware of your child's eating and weight-related attitudes and behaviors.** "Early intervention for these conditions is often critical to a more positive treatment outcome," says Mazzeo.

Eating disorders have a significant genetic component, but environment also matters, particularly when there is an underlying genetic vulnerability. Having open conversations about eating disorders, their causes, and your child's risks can help prevent future problems.

I think about how far I have come and how much I still can accomplish. Not in a dreading, 'so much work to do' kind of way heavy with depression, but with hope for the future. Excitement for what will be.

—Alison Beining

Blue Dragonfly

Alison Beining

In myth, dragonflies are the carriers for your deepest desires, dreams, and hopes. As an animal spirit totem, the dragonfly means to ask yourself to be truly mindful of your desired outcome. It means you must break through your illusions and make your dreams a reality. What you think turns into what you see; your thoughts are responsible for your physical surroundings and, in my case, your person. The dragonfly means to live life to the fullest! At least that is what I tell people when they compliment my blue dragonfly tattoo. It is only true in part.

When I was in high school, in the midst of my disorder, I would save my lunch money together and buy jewelry from this pro-ana site I was a member of named after a blue dragonfly. The site isn't around any longer. The admin went into recovery, last I heard. I hope she did; everyone deserves to find their happiness again.

And recovery is possible. It is a long, hard journey at times, but the rewards outweigh any happiness I ever felt during my ED years. I may not be fully recovered, as I still have days that are more trying than others, but it has been years since I have made myself throw up, done any kind of self-harm, or actively restricted.

I liken the creation of my eating disorder to the creation of a tornado. Not all storms progress to a tornado's force, as not all diets lead to disordered eating or distorted thoughts about food and eating. The suspicions and paranoia that followed my eating disorder were long in the making, spreading roots far into my psyche. When it comes down to it, my ED was just a matter of luck. (Or lack thereof?) The perfect storm, if you will. Heredity plays some part in it: my great grandmother battled anorexia and fought hard to maintain her weight in her golden years.

A tornado also needs the right background; a hot and cold front clashing still does not create the storm. The wind, like an unstable home life, has to be just right to force such an uncertain reaction. Even the temperature must be reactive to finally create a tornado. Otherwise it is just a storm and will pass without major damage.

Another factor contributing to my eating disorder development is Borderline Personality Disorder, which my mother has, her mother has, and I'm sure my great grandmother had. Like all bad qualities I have inherited, including weak ankles, I am also lucky enough to have BPD. The impulsive nature takes extra time and care to overcome.

Because my mother has the same disorder, my home life was unstable and extremely stressful, another building block to my ED. For it was not one single thing that led to my bulimia and self-starvation but a thousand grains of sand that fell without notice until they buried me.

Living with my unstable and often unpredictably violent mother, I became anxious and withdrawn. Even at a young age, the swift shift between perfect, doting mother and an aggressive monster made me superstitious. It was often sudden, and when it had finished, she would act like nothing had happened. With tears streaming down my face, I was left to wonder if I had gone insane and lost my mind entirely. I would lie awake at night, terrified of what else I had misconstrued in my head.

Her mood shifts brought on my constant guilt: *What had I done to create this mess? What did I say that was wrong and set her off again?* She would shout and scream at us for hours until falling blank and staying in her room for days or weeks on end. My father was a coward, leaving me to fend for myself most of the time. He drowned himself in alcohol, not solving anything at all. He was a watercolor painting that someone had dumped a bucket of water over, smearing the colors into a pastel ghost of itself.

When she was not flying off the handle, she was a perfect mother. My friends never believed the horrible stories I told them because, to the outside world, she was the ideal mother. She baked and cooked homemade meals, kept the house clean, and often greeted me with gifts and treats. We would play games and make crafts together, but that didn't last.

I recall one specific summer day when my parents fought loudly downstairs. I was inside. It was about eleven in the morning, and I had been eating breakfast before the fight started. I don't recall if they were arguing about me. But I felt such undeniable guilt that I had eaten and therefore had caused the fight. Illogical I know, but I felt an unbridled superstition that eating causes bad things to happen. So I was in my room, leaning against the door crying because I caused this fight on a seemingly perfect Sunday, and I just keep repeating in my head, *I will never eat again, I will never eat again.* In my mind not eating would prevent anything bad from happening. I also recall associating the kitchen and dining room with negative confrontations, even before my ED.

The common threads within my home life were inconsistency and instability. At times my mother would hit me, I would struggle back and a fight would ensue, but I never hit her, just to be the bigger person and to be able to say (when inevitably the police would show up, or so I thought, at least) that I never once hit her back. She was also cruel at times, telling me when I was in the throes of bulimia that I was "as ugly inside as I am on the outside." That, of course, triggered a period of starvation and self-harm. During those dark times she said the most unimaginable things.

I have blocked most memories completely; the majority of that time is lost to a dark mist I don't dare poke too often. As Alice so perfectly stated, "I'm afraid I can't explain myself, sir. Because I am not myself, you see?"

I learned growing up that no matter how sad or confusingly painful things were at home, you make polite conversation and act like it is all fine. Why dredge up something I didn't want to talk about? So I started lying. I lied about my mother and how things were at home. I stopped inviting friends over. As time went on, I went less frequently to friends' houses. It wasn't that I wanted to be home, for oftentimes I would wander the nearby cemetery or slightly abandoned train tracks with half-taken-apart trucks and school buses. I would read there and in parks, anywhere I could be alone and not think about the shit I couldn't understand then; I didn't have all the pieces to the puzzle.

The indefinable quality that contributed most to my ED, however, was active denial. If something happened I did not like, I couldn't deal with what it meant or caused. Instead of accepting the change and dealing with it like a healthy individual, I would hide it. Deny if ever confronted and lie to protect myself.

In my mind, food was my magic power. If I could control food, I could control my emotions. If I controlled food, I could think about something other than if my mother would react violently or not. My ED enabled me to live in my own world with my own distractions and goals and triumphs. As the ED progressed, it actively caused me to fail at projects I wanted to do. Not just things I deemed impossible—college, a normal life at all—but even the things that were important to me. I couldn't exercise because I was too tired. I couldn't write because I couldn't focus from the lack of food. I was flailing, doing what I could to stave the darkness inside from consuming me whole. I felt it physically, like a painful itching right beneath the skin.

"If I had a world of my own, everything would be nonsense. Nothing would be what it is, because everything would be what it isn't. And contrary wise, what is, it wouldn't be. And what it wouldn't be, it would. You see?" Another Alice quote, as I often felt as having an ED is like stepping through the looking glass and seeing everything as it was not. Even I was not as I have been, or ever would have been.

I regularly experienced cycles of mania followed by long periods of brooding depression. The days I felt like myself were rare if at all. Dissociation and body dysmorphia also plagued me, costing many school days. The obsessive, compulsive thoughts propelled my self-harm, which increased my lying. It was to the point that everything I said to everyone was a lie. Because I lived inside my head, hanging out with people forced me to act like another person than I was. Every smile, a lie. Every word that wasn't centered on food or lack of food was a lie. Even chit-chat seemed like a staged interaction. I was a character in a play of my life, but my ED was the director and writer of it.

While I lived at home, my parents were completely inept and unprepared for dealing with me, which fueled our miscommunications and problems. Even though we had gone to family therapy and I had my own therapy at separate times, they never got any information from the professionals or found it themselves. I found it a slap in the face; of course they didn't care.

One thing I recall was that my mother would purchase trigger binge food, knowing it was a trigger binge food. She would hide a box of cookies in a locked room and only keep a few in the cupboard at a time. The locked room contained other items my paranoid mother was afraid I would steal or destroy, I am not sure which. Pills she thought I might try to overdose on, at times the house phone, leaving me trapped in my own middle-class prison.

My mother also engaged in physical fights with me. She would get in my face, push all of my buttons until I lost my temper and would scream and curse as loud as I could manage. She would start something, a shove, a slap, or a punch. One time we wrestled over my purse, in which I was hiding Ipecac I had taken from a friend so she would not use it; I had never touched the stuff myself. (Ironic that I was innocent for once?) She managed to pin me, clutching my purse beneath me. She would not relent, and I was willing to die to defy her. She had a good two hundred pounds on me at the time, and she sat on me until I passed out. She wrestled my purse from my unconscious hands and left me in my room, torn apart by the brawl. I came to and for some reason never called the police.

Not only was the physical abuse unpredictable, but I associated recovery with that mindset and behavior. I had this rage I didn't know how to express. It turned inward; if my mother hated me so much, what had I done? Nothing. That must have meant everything I did was wrong.

I pushed everyone away. My first boyfriend I broke up with after a day because he hugged me. After that physical contact, I was shaking so bad I fled his house and puked on the side of the road. The saying "you can't love anyone else until you love yourself" always stuck with me, and honestly, no one person was more important than my ED.

I was at my lowest weight in freshman year; my skin was vampire pale from never eating. I always looked sick, even though I felt "healthy." Headaches and migraines plagued me constantly. I was weak from not eating, but it is difficult to determine now what was from malnutrition and what was from the heavy weight of depression. It was impossible to care about anything anymore. My BPD was out of control, unmedicated and undiagnosed at this point; I was manic and depressive, isolating myself.

My ED depended on which cycle I was in, a depressive period would lend a famine. I couldn't eat, even if I wanted to. Food was ashen; it had no taste at all, at times. When manic, I often binged and purged. I felt alive when manic; I was reckless and wondered how I never got into more trouble. If I had had access to more trouble, I'm sure I would have been much worse.

In part I believed I needed the eating disorder. I needed it to live the life I wanted as a writer. I needed it to succeed at anything. I could only find love if I was thin (later disproved!). I could only move out if I didn't eat. I held food as some sort of twisted god, and my happiness was dependent on how little I ate.

My turning point was around 21 or 22, however. I had impulsively quit my job. I did not have anything saved or lined up and only had two weeks to figure out how to pay rent. Quitting was justified because I had been severely depressed; the job involved long hours that seemed to beat my soul with every second-hand strike of the clock. It wasn't hard or complicated work, in fact it was mind-numbingly easy.

I found a new roommate, and the plan was to get myself on my feet and in a couple of months move on. I needed to leave, escape, and I had some ideas but was feeling light and free and decided I would figure it out as I went. I had my car, so I felt free, filled with hope, and open to all possibilities.

I was pursuing my dreams, and despite my backward route there, I felt pretty adult. It was the most stable I had been in years. I had my mini freakouts, yes, but overall I was taking it easier on myself. That ED voice, while still controlling me, felt less aggressive than before and more comforting, much like a superstition. I didn't feel the rushing panic as often. I felt like I could do this, at least for a while.

I felt like I was a chunk of the way down the long path to recovery. I didn't have insurance, so my options were all secondhand from my old therapy notes and things I had read about. Mindfulness has been extremely helpful. *The Lazy Guru's Guide to Life* is more insightful than it sounds, I promise you. Several books about BPD and ED recovery helped me feel better. I felt healthy mentally and had energy to learn how to change how I thought. What an impossible task!

I read a lot of mindfulness books, even dabbling in Buddhism and such things. Mindfulness taught me how to let go. I learned how to enjoy the moment and not worry when it will end, because it will end, that much is sure. But the ending does not make the moment any less sweet. Only worrying about something can sour the moment. And in the end, moments are all we really have.

It started simply at first. I read my old journals and followed a modified hospitalization regime. The diet especially was modified. I did not cheat, however; I just went slowly. I was determined to achieve recovery, and I knew it was not going to be an overnight success.

I learned how to listen to myself and not the extra bullshit around me. I learned how to make myself happy, because no one else can do that. No, I'm not a ball of sunshine every day or even most days, but I am happy.

My recovery was not completely linear, and I had setbacks. The hardest part for my recovery was letting go of the disillusioned ideals I have about weight and thinness and life in general, really. After being so caught up in my own personal drama, being social seemed strange. After spending so much time in my head focused on my own made-up world, it took weeks into recovery before I felt I had anything to talk about at all.

Everyone around me had gone about their lives for years while I essentially was frozen in time. My friends were polite and let me quietly listen to their conversations, trying to engage me when they could. I still felt like a ghost of myself with so many things swirling inside my head.

Recovery was a full-time affair, and normal things like parties and boyfriends only meant more complications. I still lied to keep up my weak facade of being the perfect Alli. I told everyone recovery was going great and I was happy to be alive.

In reality, some days were challenging, and progress involved self-evaluation and reflection. I was about 11 when I became serious about my weight. The last time I made myself purge I was 25. I am 28 now. Fourteen of my years, about half my life, was spent in this lifestyle, and I never imagined I would give it up. I assumed this was my life.

The more I argued with the ED voice, though, the softer she spoke. Each time, I told her she wasn't helping me anymore, that she was the one lying to me, not everyone else. I even wrote her a couple of letters. As my recovery progressed, I was angry at my ED for wasting so much of my time and health, for the pain it caused so many people around me, for the bridges burned and relationships scorned, for the embarrassment about everything that had happened.

Not to say I am never triggered. I have at times in the last few years been weak and looked at pro-thin pictures and let myself be tempted slightly. I let myself play out the twisted fantasy and imagine how it would go. Like someone who used to smoke cigarettes, I can taste what it was like again. Part of me yearns to go back during dark times. When I am strong, it doesn't phase me. I go long stretches with no shadows chasing my thoughts, without doing impossible caloric math in my head to value my worth.

Though the new thoughts seem like a strong riptide when they tug at me, I know they are a weak reminder of how I used to feel. "Life is too short to be depressed," someone told me in the hospital. I try to keep that in mind when I am feeling down.

The other helpful thing that has kept me in line in recovery has been my husband, well, before he was my husband, obviously.

And I don't like adding this, in part because having a relationship while suffering from an ED is not a cure or solution at all. When we became close friends, despite being drawn to him, I pushed him away because 1. How could he love a crazy like me? 2. In my entire life, no one was ever more valued or more important than my ED.

I recall lying in a hospital bed after having had surgery. My father had brought my friend up, and as they sat in my room, my father urged me to pick out something from the menu. I fidgeted and fumbled, stalled and lied about why I couldn't eat. The fact was, of course, I was scared of lying in bed and eating. My friend calmly but sternly told me, "You really should eat something." And I immediately caved and picked something from the menu. No complaining or uselessly moving it around the plate. I ate it. I forced it down and left what I thought I could get away with. It wasn't like I was severely underweight at this point. Unhealthy, yes, but not in immediate danger.

The dynamic changed with that simple phrase. I knew he cared for me, about me, without the negative bullshit that followed my thoughts on food and past food situations with my parents. He said it out of purity. It flipped my perspective of recovery. I wasn't confused or thought people were trying to trick me or make me less than I thought I was at the time. The negative experiences surrounding food, recovery, the kitchen, and dining room faded away. I never expected myself to have a healthy, normal relationship, so the fact that it fell into my lap and I didn't strangle it to death was a miracle.

For the first time ever, instead of self destructing, I had to repel my normal instinct to push him away as soon as I realized he made me vulnerable. I forced myself to push through those impulses to see what was underneath. Even the best of partners cannot win over an eating disorder if the ED individual does not want to recover. My eating disorder was a state of mind. It changed everything about my perceptions. It changed the looks people gave me and the words they said, if only in my head, because I perceived it all in a tainted lens.

As Alice said so perfectly, "I give myself very good advice but I very seldom follow it."

For the first time in my life, I needed to do what was right for my body. For the sake of my body. I had my best friend through this newest transition to help me be healthy rather than obsessive. Cooking for someone other than myself has helped me become normalized. I even cook with oil and butter now!

And the funniest thing happened. The more I listened to my body and what it needed, the easier it became. It wasn't always easy, especially after I developed a chronic pain condition. I had to take a slower pace in this abused body.

My anxiety still gets the better of me some days, but the majority of the time, I feel stronger and more stable. I wish I could tell my younger self that it will pass. The anxious, manic, skin-crawling sensation does not last forever.

When I start to feel down and my thoughts begin to spiral, I ask myself if these thoughts are productive to my goals. If I'm still being emotional and my perception is so skewed by depression and anxieties, I am not being logical. I ask myself, *if a friend came to me saying this, what would I tell them?* This thought process has really helped me change my perception relating to myself and my body and helped me avoid being overly critical or perfectionist. It has helped me see my body as an extension of my soul.

When I am feeling strong, I write down the qualities I think I have. I am kind, helpful, good at my job, well-liked, creative, good with animals, a good listener, etc. It helps to look at the list when I feel defeated and miserable, brimming with self-hate and pity.

I logically know that when I am feeling down, my perception has shifted. It is similar to a personality shift at times. When I am depressed, my entire world is flipped, and even my tastes are different. Reading over the list reminds me that I am more than my ED. I can do more with my life than binge and purge and starve. Before all of us lie infinite possibilities through recovery. I just need to shake this disease that hangs onto me like a giant wet blanket. I need to find that fire buried deep inside me, acting as my individual pilot light, keeping my soul and dreams ignited.

When I look at my dragonfly tattoo now I don't think about reaching my goal weight or how many calories I've had for the day. I think about how far I have come and how much I still can accomplish. Not in a dreading, 'so much work to do' kind of way heavy with depression, but with hope for the future. Excitement for what will be. I am proud to be nearly thirty now, excited for my future with my amazing husband who supported me through my darkest times and guided my hand through hell until we came to the other side.

You should never change yourself for anyone, but having that outside support system was invaluable. When your thoughts turn dark and no light seems possible ever again, know that it will pass. Even if it's a letter you write yourself, an outside voice can snap some reality into the underland of eating disorders.

Alli lives at home happily with her supportive husband and focuses on her writing. She recovered from bulimia with the help of an anxiety program created by Khail Kapp. Self love and recovery are possible, and everyone deserves to be this happy!

If I love myself, I know I can stay happy.

—Anonymous

Loving Myself

Anonymous

I never struggled with my weight until I was an adult. I had always been athletic; cheerleading, basketball, and volleyball kept me fit and busy all year long.

That all changed when I turned 23 and became pregnant with my first child. I was not yet married, but we had planned to wed. We just had not planned to have a baby so soon. It was quite a surprise, and it led to two of the craziest years of my life.

In 2003, when my daughter was just three months old, my husband of less than a year and I were both told we had to move to Houston, TX to keep our jobs. We spent our one-year wedding anniversary with a new baby in a new city far away from home where we knew no one. My first bout of depression set in, and I began to eat my feelings.

During the first three months in our new location, I gained 30 pounds and looked pregnant again. I felt tired all the time and sad most every day, and I desperately wanted my friends and family. Though it was a challenging time, we decided to have another baby. I got pregnant right away and stopped eating those feelings because I spent day and night nauseous and vomiting. I knew pregnancy was going to be rough, but I never imagined how bad it would get.

After we had lived in Houston for only nine months, my husband told me he had found a new job back home. I didn't even know he was looking for another job, so I wasn't yet prepared to go back. I spent the next month frantically trying to find a new job in our hometown. I found a job quickly, but I ended up taking a pay cut for a horrible clerk job that I hated. I was miserable in my pregnancy, and now I was miserable in my

179

job. For the first time ever, I began to resent my new husband. I felt hurt and left out that he had never told me his plans to find a new job. I felt like my voice did not matter to him.

At 36 weeks pregnant, I woke up feeling very strange. I got dressed, dropped off my daughter at my parent's house, and made my way to work. I soon realized I had not felt the baby move for several hours, which was unusual. I called the doctor and was told to go to the hospital right away. The ultrasound showed no heartbeat. My world was shattered, and I have never really recovered. The loss set me on a highly destructive path of overeating and binge eating.

Everyone grieves differently, but it took me a long time to learn that lesson. I was furious that my husband did not seem as devastated as I was. While caring for my toddler, I spent my days crying and eating. Over the next six months I gained over 50 pounds. I did not even care. I had given up on myself.

My husband never ate healthily or worked out, so naturally I let these things fall by the wayside. Takeout, fried foods, pizza, and sweets became my four major food groups.

Then my husband began to pull away. The intimacy completely stopped. He would not touch me or kiss me unless I initiated it, but most of the time he shut me down with some excuse. Around the same time, he began to work nights and weekends voluntarily. He did bring in more money, but by this time we both had better jobs, and I no longer lived paycheck to paycheck. I feared he was working more to avoid being home with our toddler and me, but I could never get him to talk to me.

After I spent months trying to talk to him, he finally told me the truth. He told me he was no longer attracted to me. After that, the bingeing got worse. By then, I was 100 lbs. overweight. I hated myself, and my confidence was nil. The one bright spot was my new job. I consider myself smarter than the average bear, so I never faltered in believing in my intellectual abilities. It was the one thing I had left.

A few years later, I had the opportunity to join management. I took my promotion later that year and threw myself into my work. The job itself was stressful, though, and perpetuated my already-established unhealthy relationship with food. I did not drink, I did not smoke, I did not do drugs. My vice was food. A lot of it.

When my husband worked late (still), I would sit down and comfort myself with food after my daughter went to bed. I knew it was wrong, and I knew it made me feel terrible not only physically but emotionally as well. I just could not stop. Food was my friend, my comfort.

Even after my husband and I started working the same hours, we spent little time together. We fell into a pattern of eating in front of the TV. Then I would help my daughter with her bedtime routine and retire to the bedroom alone to watch TV and eat my hidden snacks. We did this every night of the week. We were nothing more than roommates with a child in the middle. Most nights after eating my stash, I would sit there and think about how much I hated myself and how I needed to make changes. I knew what I needed to do; I just could not find it in myself to change my habits.

Since my husband and I were both working days, I began to work late. The work was endless, but, mostly, I just did not want to go home. Maybe I wanted him to experience the pain and loneliness I felt when he worked nights and weekends and left me home alone with our daughter. So, most nights, I stayed in the office until 9 pm. For dinner I bought snacks from the vending machines or walked to the McDonald's next door.

A few years later, I accepted my second promotion, which involved traveling to Dallas for two weeks each month for six months. The first week I spent in Dallas I met some great people and had fun. Not once in Dallas did I binge or overeat, although at the time I didn't even notice. During the second week of that first month, a group of us hung out every night after class. We went to happy hours and dinners, and the problems of the real world began to melt away. Again, still no bingeing or overeating in Dallas, and I even refrained from bingeing at home.

While traveling, I became good friends with one man in particular. We seemed to have so much in common, and we just clicked right away. He was also a natural flirt, but I never thought twice about him in a romantic way. I was an extremely overweight married woman. Why would he be flirting with me? I decided he did not mean anything by it and was just having fun, so I flirted back.

It felt so good to talk and laugh with a member of the opposite sex. Early on, we had a conversation about what was happening between us. He admitted he really liked me, and I told him the same. I felt flabbergasted that he would want me at all. My husband certainly did not want me, and I did not love myself either. I didn't even feel comfortable in my own skin. We agreed to never act on our attraction, though, because he was married as well.

This man and I talked daily. The emotional affair was absolutely intoxicating; I had not received this kind of attention in years. The first time we slept together I was nervous about the whole thing. We knew it was wrong, but we could not help it. And it was amazing! It quickly turned into a full-fledged affair that occurred only when we were in Dallas. Not once did my husband question me about why I always went early. I was prepared with a lie, but I did not even need it.

By the end of my time in Dallas, I had dropped a significant amount of weight and was so proud of myself! I began to like my new curves and how I looked in my clothes. I felt a confidence I had not felt since I was 20 years old. When I realized why I had lost the weight, I felt both happy and sad at the same time. I was happy that I had my confidence back, that I had more energy and felt comfortable in my own skin. I was sad, though, that I had let myself get so caught up in what others think of me, especially the two men in my life. One lifted me up, and the other brought me down, but why did I let that happen? No one else is responsible for my happiness except me.

Despite the new me, things still felt wrong at home. Here was the man I married who did not really talk to me, was not interested in what I was doing or had to say, and rarely touched me or was intimate with me in any way. I just could not do it anymore. On the other side, there was a man who loved everything about me, even when I was obese. He loved me for me and not just what I looked like on the outside.

Knowing I deserved to be with someone who was good for me and not toxic was eye-opening. Did I leave my husband? Yes, I did. Did I leave him for the other man? Nope. He and I had many talks and decided to end the affair. He did not want to leave his wife, and I respected him for that. Although it was amicable, I was still hurt, but I refused to fall back into binge eating and see my body go in the wrong direction again. I knew by then that no other person was going to dictate how I felt about myself.

I still had to tell myself this daily because I was heartbroken to lose these men. Yes, I wanted to eat all day every day during that time. I stayed on track, though, and because of that I felt I finally had power. I learned things about myself and my significant other and about what I want and feel I deserve in life.

I want someone who will walk beside me and not leave me trailing ten steps behind all the time. I want someone who has an interest in me and pushes me to be my best and supports me in everything. I deserve that. The affair taught me that there are people out there who can love me for who I am and not what I look like.

Within six months, I was divorced and living on my own. My now ex-husband never really put up a fight when I told him I wanted a divorce, so that confirmed I was doing the right thing for my daughter and for me. The fact that he didn't even want to try cut deeply, but I think things were too far gone between us, and I could not really blame him.

I never told anyone about that affair, but it has made me a better person. It made my binge eating disorder disappear. I began to value myself so much more, so in turn, I valued how I treated my body.

It has been over four years since my last binge-eating session. I am still single and have not had much time to look for someone else, but I am okay with that. I want to get my daughter through high school and off to college and finish my own degree.

In the meantime, I continue to take care of myself, mentally and physically, and I make sure my daughter knows to never settle for someone. I always tell her to hold out for that one person who values her in every way and loves her for who she is. I also encourage her to be with someone because she *wants* to be with them and not because she *needs* them financially or otherwise. Most importantly, I tell her to love herself no matter what.

If I love myself, I know I can stay happy. Eating better and exercising regularly keeps me happy and confident. And yes, when I am alone, I still frequently think about sitting down to eat a whole pizza, but I never want to go back to the person I was before. It is just not worth it.

Know that whatever a psychological disorder has prevented you from doing in the past, you can achieve it later in life. And it will be all the sweeter for it.

—MJ Mars

Graduation

MJ Mars

When I look back, I suppose I have always had issues with food. For me, food was not something to be enjoyed. It was an essential inconvenience, as perfunctory as going to the toilet, and with the same bashful undertones. In some ways, eating was as intimate as a sexual act. I spent my early teens choosing the blandest of foods or bashfully waving at a sandwich at a café checkout so the staff member could read the label without me having to say the words aloud. People knowing what I wanted to put inside me and what I desired left me feeling inexplicably ashamed.

Perhaps these food issues stem from my childhood. When I was eight, my father left my mother. In reality, my sister and I were perfectly happy with his sudden disappearance. He had been a sullen, antagonistic figure in our household for a long while, and his violent outbursts, which usually preceded the beating of our faithful Labrador, had made us all too happy to keep out of his way. I remember clearly his departure from the family home: I was watching the afternoon showing of *Neighbours* on the television as he drove away without a word. I remained glued to the set, the trials and tribulations of the residents of Ramsey Street more a concern than those playing out in my own residence.

My father remained a distant and strange figure after that. My sister and I were forced to visit him at his mother's home, where he told us how awful our mother was and showed us photographs his hired private eye had taken of her with her new boyfriend. It was all extremely tiresome, and we couldn't wait to get back to our own home after each visit, his absence all the more celebrated the stranger his behavior became.

But then things changed. When he started dating a new woman, his careful attacks against my mother became more calculated. Suddenly we were showered with compliments. We were treated to gifts, his new wife taking us out and buying us nice underwear and face products I had never even known existed. She had two beautiful daughters who were older than my sister and me, and we looked at them with awe, hopeful that one day we might look as good as they did.

Visiting my father became fun. He would take me aside and tell me things I thought I wanted to hear. When I'd had an argument with Mum, I was told, "Well, you know it's because she loves your sister more than you. She doesn't want you around; she just wants to be with her boyfriends, and you're in the way." He would end these pep-talks with, "But I love you the most. You always have me."

His favorite game was trying to turn me against my mum, paying no mind to the fact that I spent the majority of my time with her feeling like an unwanted outcast. It seemed like the aim of the game for him was getting at my mother—a strange revenge for a crime she hadn't committed. The lies grew, and with them came a constant uncertainty. I had never been self-assured, but I began to feel disgusted with my appearance.

I remember walking through a busy shopping center when I was around twelve and bowing my head because I thought everybody was looking at me and thinking I was too ugly to show my face. I easily recall the sensation of my heart racing, the shameful heat of self-loathing pulsing through me as I scurried past the crowds. It was a feeling I would come to know well and a feeling that grew with my disorder.

The turning point with my father came when I believed his lies so fully I decided the best thing would be to move in with him. I told my mum what I was going to do, and she was obviously devastated. But as she had throughout his charades, she decided to take a step back and let things unfold. I went to my father and proudly told him I had decided to move in with him. Since he was always telling me how much he loved and wanted me, I didn't see the possibility that he might say no.

Interestingly, coward that he is, he never did say no. He just didn't say anything else. My mother contacted him repeatedly at my bidding, trying to finalize the big move. His silence was deafening. I remember the horrible truth dawning on me. Instead of going to him, I asked my mother, "He doesn't want me to move in with him, does he?" She said sadly, "I don't think so darling, no."

After that, I would spend my time at his house playing on the computer upstairs, too angry to fall back into the old routine. I was on to him, after all. Soon, he began to berate me for disappearing upstairs, and I was forced to hang out with him downstairs in mutual sullen silence. He knew he could no longer continue his abuse towards my mother. After all, she wanted me to live with her. He could no longer pretend he was better than her.

Instead, he tried to undermine my sister. But like I said, I was on to his game. One evening, over fish and chips, he began talking about her in a nasty way (all because she was older and wiser than me and had cut most ties to him months previously). I stood up and told him I was not going to listen to him talk about my sister that way. He flew into one of his rages, but I stood calm and firm. I was absolutely done with his crap. In a final fit of pique, he shouted, "You walk, and you'll be walking a long time before you see me again."

Never a truer word was said. Our only contact in the months that followed came from a post-it note attached to the paltry maintenance check that read in angry, all-caps scrawl, "HOPE YOU ARE OK," and a sinister call from his wife in which she coldly told me I needed to stop my nonsense because *he* was upset. Well, I was upset, too, not that I would ever admit it.

Years of being told he was the only person in the world who really loved and valued me had sunk in deeper than I had realised. Suddenly I was completely cast adrift. His lies had always made me suspicious of my mother's constant, steady, and *real* love, and my self-esteem was at an all-time low.

Then I went to college and loved my first year. But in my second year, the cracks began to show. I skipped classes and drank too much during the day, a period of misspent youth that gave me great pool-playing skills I still take pleasure in demonstrating every once in a while.

Then came my first panic attack. I was watching college friends perform in a play when suddenly I felt worse than I ever had. I staggered to the toilets, sure I was going to throw up, but being in the quiet and empty white-tiled bathroom somehow made the symptoms disappear. I tried to return to my seat about five times, only to be hit by the same wall of sickness every time I ventured back into the auditorium. I had no idea what was happening, but it was a feeling I would experience daily for the next three years.

The following Monday at the train station (I caught the train to college each day), my legs suddenly felt as though they wouldn't work. In the end I had to call my mum to pick me up and take me home. I thought I had some strange virus that only gave me symptoms if I was in a public place, but all too soon the racing heart and sickness became constant. It would even come on at home when I sat watching television. It would start as soon as I woke in the morning and be with me when I lay in bed unable to sleep. I became terrified I would throw up in public. It was a fear that seems irrational, but it was unshakable, and it held with it a sensation of doom.

For people reading this who have thrown up in front of people without batting an eyelid, this may sound like a bizarre fear. I know, I've met so many of you! But for me, a person who was trapped in a shame cycle that left me feeling ugly and revolting at the best of times, the thought of disgracing myself even further by showing people the contents of my insides was too much to bear.

Then it began. Two and two came together, and the shame of eating merged completely with the phobia of throwing up (which I later learned in treatment is called emetophobia and is more common than people think!).

I ate nothing but antacid chews and drank water when I needed to go out, unable to bear the idea of eating before college or travel. For me, eating would bring on sickness. There were no two ways about it. If I ate, I would throw up. So, for a long while, I didn't really eat. When I did eat, safe and sound at home and knowing I had nowhere to go, it would be the blandest, safest food imaginable.

At that time, flavor was danger. Sauces were a no-no. If I was left with a taste in my mouth from anything I consumed, I would panic, certain I would become sick. I managed to scrape through college, which was astounding given my attendance record and poor showing at final coursework. I got into university and spent the summer working days in a pub. I made new friends and was invited out in the evenings after work.

This was initially problematic, of course. But, I developed a solution. I began a cycle of minimal eating, followed by purging, which made me feel like I had too little in my stomach to get sick when I was out. Drinking alcohol also helped. When drinking, my nerves eased for a while. My constant racing heart and nausea faded into the background. I pretty much lived off antacid tablets, water, and beer for a whole summer. I am astonished I made it through.

During that time I was extremely conscious of my body. My issues with body image went hand-in-hand with my phobia of throwing up, as most psychological issues do. I took the term 'a flat stomach' extremely literally. I would constantly engage in micro-crunches, tensing the muscles of my stomach hundreds of times a day in the hope that the combination of starvation and Callanetics would somehow turn me into a worthwhile human being.

The panic over being sick affected two very important elements of the university experience: arriving there and sitting in lectures. My university was a fifty-minute bus ride from my house, the journey taking me through the countryside enshrouded A6 from Preston to Lancaster. The landscape there is absolutely lovely. The only problem was, I would usually only make it so far before I had to jump off the bus in the middle of nowhere. So, I would trudge home, sometimes walking for hours. When I think about it now, it seems crazy, the idea of walking home in all weathers down the A6. The next bus home would pass me, but there was usually no chance I could hope to get on it. Once the sick feeling came, I couldn't get rid of it. I could only ever hope that tomorrow would be a better day. It rarely was.

If I ever actually plucked up the courage to attend class, I would find a seat at the end of the aisle and near the door, but in no time I would be overwhelmed by the panicked sensation of sickness and have to run out.

Because I missed so many classes, I was hauled through disciplinaries at university, which only made things worse. I felt nothing but shame. I couldn't explain to them why I wasn't attending my classes because to admit it was to admit I was not okay. That I deserved to be thought of as unworthy and stupid and ugly and all of the other negative things I had learned to think about myself. To keep it all inside felt like the only way to be strong. To stand a chance of turning it all around one day. Of course, that never happened, and I was withdrawn from the university due to non-attendance.

Ironically, in the spherical way the world seems to operate sometimes, I now work for a university advising students on how to submit extenuating circumstances (EC) claims, amongst other things. Many of the students who use the service are unable to complete their assignments or attend their exams because of emotional problems such as mine. I sometimes wonder whether things would have been different if ECs had been available when I was a student, but I feel deep down that I still wouldn't have used them. I had to be strong, after all. How wrong I was.

Things started to settle down for me surreptitiously, really. I didn't notice a sudden change. I had treatment, such as antidepressant tablets that I stopped taking of my own accord, hypnotherapy that didn't work as I was far too guarded to relax, and general counseling that was okay but seemed fake to me. I remember talking to the therapist and being completely aware that they were probably bored, going through the motions and saying the same things they say to ten different people every day. I would encourage anyone to try these avenues, however, as they do work for many people and probably did contribute to my becoming well in the end.

My greatest influence, though, was my best friend. I met her when I started my first job in administration at a financial management company in town. She is the most matter-of-fact, bullheaded person I have ever met, and she is absolutely wonderful. When we met, her family was going through a terrible time as her mother had battled pancreatic cancer for eight years in a remarkable display of strength and courage. They all had every right to wallow and feel sorry for themselves, but they never did. They constantly looked forward rather than back, and, because of their resilience and refusal to ruminate, they were an incredibly positive influence on me.

My friend and I began to spend more time together outside of work, going to shows and out for meals. I gradually found I was putting myself into situations that before I wouldn't have been able to deal with, such as sitting in the middle of the cinema or theatre. At first I would panic all the way through, my heart racing non-stop in my chest. Sometimes I would leave the show and not remember a word of what I had just seen, but I had sat through it without running, and that was a huge victory to me.

Soon these small triumphs grew into greater tests of will. I would eat before going out without purging. I would choose to eat something like chilli and not freak out that I could taste it in my mouth as we clothes-shopped after lunch. I even managed a particularly nightmarish train journey back from a concert during which I felt sick. I was fully aware that a few years previously I would have stranded myself, unable to think of getting on the train, or would have jumped off at a stop part way home.

When I settled down in my first home, I started to enjoy cooking. Trying out recipes and flavors gave me a sense of accomplishment and pleasure. Suddenly food became something to enjoy, rather than a grim task that had to be endured. I also took pleasure in building a bit of muscle tone rather than starving myself skinny. I began to understand that when I ate well and kept active, the sick feeling all but disappeared. I had been in a vicious cycle for years, eating nothing and feeling weak and sick, all because I was afraid to eat in case I felt sick.

It seems crazy to me now that this person I am writing about was really me. I have been healthy and happy for a number of years. I eat well and am less ashamed by both my body and the food I put into it. I fulfilled my dream of becoming a writer, publishing a number of short stories.

I still have my moments, but I understand those feelings better now. By stepping away from them instead of being immersed in them as I was, I can see these feelings for what they are. They don't have the same control over me as they used to.

I wanted to share my story to encourage anyone out there who has issues with eating that it will get better one day. Those tiny little changes that lead to recovery may already have begun. You will get better. Always look forward and be proud of the small victories because they truly do lead to a wonderful life.

An eating disorder and phobia ruined my teens and caused me to drop out of university, but in October 2017 I picked up my English Literature Degree from the Open University. There were a lot of smiles on stage that day as we crossed to receive our awards, but I don't know if there were any as big as mine. Knowing that I wouldn't have even been able to sit in the auditorium a few years before, let alone be able to cross the stage in front of hundreds of people, was incredibly moving.

Know that whatever a psychological disorder has prevented you from doing in the past, you can achieve it later in life. And it will be all the sweeter for it.

Never believe this is all you are and all you will ever be. That is just the disease talking. And you are better than that.

MJ Mars has a passion for horror writing and has recently been published by Colors in Darkness in their Deadly Bargains *compilation and* Silver Empire's Secret Stairs Anthology, *which was number one in the Amazon horror chart for six weeks. MJ has also been published by Lycan Valley press, and has placed and been published in numerous writing competition publications, such as* The Stringybark Prize, Momaya, Write France, *and* Cazart. *Her work was featured in the charity anthology* Writers for Animals *published by Bridge House. She lives in Lancaster, UK, where she regularly takes inspiration from the gruesome history of the city!*

A Parent's Story of Hope

Beth Ayn Stansfield, M.Ed.

After a long embrace, I wave goodbye and watch my daughter board a plane for Colorado. It's a surreal moment; it actually brings a tear to my eye. Seven years ago, if someone had told me my daughter would be going off to college on her own, 1,660 miles away from home, I would have said they were crazy. Yes, this is a story of hope for parents and caregivers wondering if recovery is really possible.

As my daughter moved through elementary school, an eating disorder was something I certainly did not foresee in her future. Although she presented as a perfectionistic, harm-avoidant people pleaser, she remained engaged. She was well-liked by her friends both at school and at church. She played an instrument in the school band. She focused on her studies and received academic awards for her achievements. Teachers would often comment on what a pleasure it was to have her in their classes. Eerily perfect.

I do recall our relationship being somewhat uncanny, difficult to describe. I was an extroverted mother who loved her daughter and encouraged her to embrace life and take risks, yet I was unable to get her to leave my side. One who didn't know better would have easily labeled the relationship as enmeshed. I had no way to know she was suffering from social anxiety, which seemed to haunt her since birth. If I had known then what I know now, maybe, just maybe, I could have dodged what was about to turn into five years of hell for my daughter.

Following a bout with what had been initially identified as one of the rare cases of whooping cough in our state, things began to crumble for my daughter, who at that point was in middle school. Unable to function due to a constant cough, lack of sleep, and weakness as a result of her loss of appetite, she was assigned to homebound instruction. Unfortunately, the three months did not lead to resolve. We patiently revisited the specialists who then determined she was suffering from social anxiety, presenting itself as a persistent cough. Relieved to have a diagnosis, something we thought medication and a few visits to a therapist could alleviate, she returned to school.

"It is so good to see you," "We missed you," and "You lost weight" are the three responses I vividly remember hearing as she entered the doors of her school when she was able to return. What resonates in my mind the most was the comment, "You lost weight." In fact, she had lost weight, enough for folks to take notice. It wasn't even two weeks upon her re-entry to school that she made the announcement she was going to start eating "healthy" and exercising. Now, writing this, I ask myself the question, *How could I have missed the obvious?*. But, at that time, healthy eating had become the norm, and running was encouraged. I was actually excited to hear she wanted to join the cross country team. I had been a runner most of my life.

My daughter's "healthy" eating eventually became a preoccupation with food. Looking back, it was subtle—her narrowing of food groups and reducing portion sizes. Her excuses for skipping meals and outbursts at the table became more frequent. What started as a "healthy" diet was now an excuse not to eat at all. Daily weigh-ins and constant calorie counting soon followed. The running that I mentioned was now an obsession. There was no enjoyment, only a self-inflicted requirement.

Oddly, she had enough stamina to stay engaged in extracurricular activities and continue her rigorous studies at school. Outwardly, she seemed happy to those in her inner circle. A journal entry she shared with me years later read, "You know my name but not my story." And, indeed, I did not know her story. The scars I later discovered on her wrists and our deteriorating relationship suggested she was not in a good space. I no longer recognized the daughter who had clung to me for so many years. She spent the majority of her time in her room. We no longer shared lively conversations or fun times. With hollow eyes, she would gaze over me when I made mention of any concerns I had about food, lack of sleep, or her pervasive mood swings. I was very scared. It was as if something had taken over her mind.

With urgency I met with her pediatrician, who in addition to noticing her complacency, also reported an extreme fluctuation in weight. On that day, my daughter was diagnosed with an eating disorder. Following a myriad of questions, we discovered that her relationship with food trumped everything. Her weight was the most important thing in her life. As our pediatrician continued to probe, it became apparent that my daughter needed immediate help. I knew that her disposition had changed and her weight had taken a drastic turn. But an eating disorder? We were fortunate our doctor was well connected and able to get us in touch with the right providers.

We secured a treatment team of eating disorder specialists who were considered the best in our community. Her team consisted of a registered dietitian, therapist, psychiatrist, and pediatrician. Initially, I thought recruiting this team would be the answer I was looking for. Surely, they would "cure" my daughter. I would get my kid back. I was wrong. She was not responding. Often, she would refuse to attend the appointments, leaving me to sit with the specialist. On those rare occasions when she agreed to meet, my previously well-behaved daughter would make inappropriate comments and abruptly leave their offices, slamming the door behind her.

I was not familiar with eating disorders and all they entailed. But I did realize that my daughter's brain had been hijacked. She was crippled by an illness that had taken her prisoner. Dr. Cynthia Bulik, a researcher and expert in the field of eating disorders, coined the phrase "genes load the gun, and the environment pulls the trigger." I couldn't agree more. My daughter was genetically loaded, and then an event took place that set the eating disorder in motion. The disorder wasn't my fault, nor was it a willful act on her part. She did not choose to be ill.

Recognizing that she was not responding to her home-based treatment team, I decided it was time to consider a higher level of care. For us, it took a matter of three months to make that determination. With that decision made, I took the bold step to fly her to one of the most highly respected treatment facilities in the United States. This meant leaving my younger daughter with her grandparents, taking a leave of absence from work, and living 1,660 miles away from home for three months. Yes, we boarded a plane for Denver, Colorado. Not an easy trip the first time out. My daughter was in complete denial. She could not see that she was slowly killing herself.

Even with the best treatment, it is not easy. Those involved have to make mindful decisions each day to keep their eyes on recovery. At times, I grew tired, frustrated, and resentful. I cried a lot. It was the toughest thing I had ever experienced. But, after each turn, I would regroup. My daughter needed me to be strong. This is an illness that requires constant, consistent, loving support. And, truth be told, my experiences paled in comparison to what my daughter had to endure each day to make recovery happen. Have you ever felt the pain of frostbite? That time when you come in from the cold just to experience more dreadful suffering. Then, at the very moment when you think you can't take anymore there is a warm rush of heat that covers your body? For me, that seems to best describe the process of recovery.

Treatment for an eating disorder is simple. Eat. Food is medicine. Unfortunately, I discovered very quickly, it was not that easy. My daughter had developed a preoccupation with food, making dieting the most important thing in her life. To introduce her to three meals and three snacks a day was like speaking a foreign language. And, to say she couldn't run until she was weight restored was not an easy feat. So, the kitchen became the battleground. There were many arguments and meals met with silence. We both endured. With the help of her treatment providers, I learned to challenge her resistance, and she developed a toolbox of skills to help her manage the anxiety. The days ticked by. Over time, I started to notice less resistance and more conversation. I was starting to get my girl back.

Recovery does not happen overnight; it takes years. I think the term flexible recovery is most accurate. It's not a straight line from start to finish. Recovery comes with hiccups, sometimes with small lapses and sometimes full-blown setbacks. When my daughter required a second round of treatment in Denver, I recall a vocal parent who rose abruptly from his seat in one of our support groups. While pointing his finger firmly in my direction, with fear in his voice, he loudly declared "I am not going to be you." The room went silent. You could hear a pin drop. Without hesitation, I assured him that I understood. I don't know whatever happened to that family. My hope is that he wasn't sitting in my seat two years later. But, if so, it's okay. Setbacks are sometimes a part of recovery. Whatever it takes to get to the finish line.

In this journey, I found that I was a lot tougher than I had given myself credit for being. I found that I was stronger than an eating disorder. I found that through the darkest times, God put the right people in the right place at the right time in my life so that I could be there for my daughter. One of those individuals told me, "One day your daughter is going to thank you for this." That registered dietitian in Denver, Colorado will never know how I clung to those words for years.

My daughter just boarded a plane for Colorado, this time not for treatment but to complete her undergraduate degree in psychology. After that long embrace and that wave good-bye, she yelled to me, "Thank you, mom."

I wish I had a crystal ball to tell you the exact date that your loved one will be where my daughter is in life. Recovery looks different for everyone. What I can tell you, however, is that times are changing. Research is at its all-time best for eating disorders. There is hope.

Educate yourself. Find a local support group. Take care. And know that full recovery is possible.

Beth Ayn Stansfield, M.Ed., spent 35+ years in the field of education as an educator, a counselor, a behavioral specialist, and an administrator. In addition, she served as adjunct faculty at Virginia Commonwealth University in their Department of Education. While supporting her daughter through recovery, Beth Ayn discovered a new calling when she met an unmet need—helping individuals, families, and professionals connect with supports and resources by way of eating disorders.

With a vision to provide services across the Commonwealth of Virginia, Beth Ayn created Stay Strong Virginia. Much of her work can be found at www.staystrongvirginia.org. She also provides presentations, facilitates support groups, creates monthly e-newsletters, offers quarterly community events, and is in the process of writing/publishing her first book.

I let go of my perceived control over my life and finally believed that the methods of controlling my food intake or harming my body were not tools of safety, but of imprisonment.

—Krista Hutcherson

She Feeds on Ashes

Krista Hutcherson

I once listened to a cunning voice inside me that told me being thin would make me special, beautiful, loved, and safe. It lured me into believing it as it firmly placed its two hands on either side of my face and directed my focus to a consuming obsession with being thin. It gradually chewed me up and swallowed me, piece by piece, muting my spirit and voice and obscuring it with its own stealthy lies. But it wasn't always this way.

I grew up in a stable, supportive, loving, Christian home. My parents are still married, I have a great relationship with my younger brother, I am close to my sister-in-law, and I adore my two nephews. We are a close-knit family. I have many wonderful childhood memories of going to the beach with my family, riding my bike around our neighborhood, and swinging on my wooden swing in the backyard. I was a leader among my neighborhood friends and regularly wrote and organized plays, puppet shows, carnivals, book clubs, and other fun adventures. I made up gymnastic routines on my balance beam with my friend next door and wrote stories and poetry in our backyard hammock for hours. I was unusually shy at school but still had a small group of friends whose birthday parties and sleepovers I attended. My world felt safe and happy.

I first remember comparing my body to another girl's and falling short in my eyes when I was taking gymnastics (which I loved!) in the fourth grade. One day, I noticed my thighs were bigger than some of the other girls' and there was no space between mine like there was with theirs. Those girls were long and graceful, and, for the first time, I felt bulky and cumbersome. I began to enjoy gymnastics less and less as I compared my body with the other gymnasts'. I eventually told my mom I wasn't interested in taking the classes any longer, and she was certainly fine with that because they were expensive.

I don't remember struggling much with my body image after that until I left elementary school to attend a large, intimidating, two-story middle school. I was faced with an entirely new group of kids who all seemed to have this secret code for what clothes to wear and what words to say to fit in and be accepted. I wasn't interested in the things these kids talked about, and I didn't laugh at their jokes. I played the violin in orchestra (which, in my school, was NOT cool!) and frequently read a book by myself at the lunch table. I was often bullied and felt my spirit shrink gradually beneath the jeers and taunts from my peers. I began to believe there was something wrong with me, with my hair, my clothes, my body, and my personality. I escaped regularly into my imagination, finding solace in books, music, and my love of writing.

Around this time, a relative began sexually abusing me on and off for about two years. The combination of the rejection from my peers and the confusing, shameful experience of being touched inappropriately multiple times by a family member birthed lies in my mind that profoundly affected my sense of self-worth. Depression crept up inside me like a quiet shadow and wrapped its thin, empty arms around my shoulders to cloak me in despair, defeat, worthlessness, and hopelessness. My seemingly solid foundation of a Christian home and happy childhood began to reveal cracks that crept like spider webs across my sense of identity.

As I entered puberty, my body began to change in ways for which I was not prepared. When I got my period, my mom congratulated me because I was now a woman. I remember thinking that if this was what came along with being a woman, I wanted to be a little girl again. During that period of time, a classmate commented that the pants size I was wearing was way too large for a girl of my short stature. Her words stripped me to my bones, and I felt humiliated and exposed. I went home and got on the scale. As I looked at the numbers on the scale I felt the little girl in me drain away, and with her, all my childhood happiness.

It wasn't long before an eating disorder sunk its claws into me. Soon, every waking moment was spent thinking about my body, food, calories, and weight loss. The insanity, distortion, darkness, and hopelessness of an eating disorder is difficult to articulate. My words feel insufficient to describe the monster that took over my life and intended to devour me whole.

As I entered my teen years, my parents unintentionally discouraged me from expressing my anger to them by scolding me for "talking back." They have long since apologized for this response and admitted it was influenced by their own inability to deal with conflict in a healthy way because of their own upbringings. Later, when I was in counseling for the eating disorder, my parents even bought me a punching bag to help me release my anger. But I somehow believed that letting out my anger was weak. I believed if they knew I was angry it would give them power over me. And so I suppressed any negative feelings I had, along with my voice. Eating and then throwing up became a way out for me, a backdoor for those negative emotions to be released, a violent scream for all I wanted to say but couldn't.

One night, my dad heard me throwing up in the bathroom after dinner, and he confronted me. I lied and made up some excuse, but he knew that something was wrong. He contacted my youth pastor because he knew that I trusted him. The pastor had already explained to me he would need to tell my parents about the abuse, and he did. This was the beginning of a long line of counselors my parents sent me to in the hopes of rescuing their daughter from herself.

Even as my body became smaller and my behavior became more obsessive, I was unable to see myself accurately through my own eyes. It was as if I was looking through a distorted pair of lenses of a funhouse mirror that warped my vision and caused me to see myself as fat. No matter how much I restricted my food intake and purged, no matter how low the numbers on the scale read, it was never enough.

When I was 16 years old, I found acceptance in the punk rock crowd at my school. I began to build a new foundation based on my new punk identity paired with my eating disorder. I shaved the underside of my head, dyed my hair purple, and began to dress creatively in the clothes I wanted to wear instead of always trying to fit in with everyone else. I believed the old Krista was weak, vulnerable, timid, fat, and always out of control. She was naïve and trusted everybody. She was lonely and alone.

The new Krista was thin and strong and in control. She was knowledgeable, tough, daring, skeptical, and NOT vulnerable. The truth was that I was extremely vulnerable to the stealthiest and filthiest lies whispering in my head that I was unlovable and weak and that being thin would make me lovable, strong, and safe. In reality, I was not in control at all. The eating disorder had taken over my life and was in control of me. I could not take a bite, look at myself in the mirror, or be around other people without it demeaning me and demanding I obey its every command. It drove my every decision like a slave master, hurling its insults and whipping me into submission every minute of my life.

I was always hungry and always tired. I slept all day for ten to twelve hours at a time and dreamt about enjoying feasts of glorious foods without guilt or fear, only to wake up ashamed, a failure for giving in to my urge to eat in my sleep.

Even as the rules for eating and losing weight became more strict within my mind, I began to become increasingly attracted to risky behavior, seemingly intent on self-destruction. I began to experiment with drugs and alcohol and abandoned myself in relationships to guys, believing I was dirty and used and worthless so it didn't matter what they did to me. Recklessly, I flung out my needy heart, riddled with open, gaping holes, in an attempt to absorb any semblance of love into myself, an enormous, depthless vacuum.

I mentally begged each boy to fill me up: *please someone love me*. But each boy I chose to be with was fighting his own demons. They eagerly took my heart, pressed it greedily to their own to suck the life out of it in an attempt to sustain their own hearts. And when I wasn't enough for them, they hurled my heart to the ground in frustration, stomped on it, and crushed it beneath their boots. Then they gave it back to me, limp and shredded and emptier than before. I shamefully gathered up the pieces and shoved them back inside of me, only to offer them again to the next boy, heavy like a sponge with hope and longing and desperation. They abused me emotionally, mentally, and sexually, but I didn't even think it was abuse because they weren't hitting me. I believed I was worthless and deserved to be treated as such. And each time I was abused, yet again, the lies were reinforced until they became a part of my bones, my skin.

Each night, I cried myself to sleep. I spent all my wakeful hours obsessing over calories and food intake and dragging myself through life like the living dead. I did not believe I would make it to my 21st birthday. I prayed to God each night to end my misery and my life and to let me live in heaven with Him, away from this nightmare. But every day, I woke up again.

Though I frequently skipped classes and couldn't concentrate when I did attend, I somehow graduated high school and was accepted into college. I barely made it a year before flunking out because I stopped going to my classes. I was sleeping all day and hanging out with my friends at night, my mind bent on self-destruction. After being home from college for several months, I found a website called "Something Fishy."

This was a time when the Internet was still fairly new and no one knew about blogging. It was a site dedicated to encouraging girls who were trying to overcome an eating disorder. I found hundreds of posts by girls who were in the midst of the disorder or in recovery, and I spent hours scrolling through them to read the words that were like a lifeline to me. I told my mom I couldn't imagine being able to eat normally and not obsess over my weight, to be free of all this like so many of those girls claimed they were. It was incredible. It felt impossible to ever be rid of this bondage, to live without this constant war in my head, but I clung to their words and tucked them into a secret place inside my chest, where new hope shimmered a faint glow among the darkness and wreckage.

Before long, my parents arranged for me to go to a treatment center for eating disorders in Arizona. I was 19 years old. They told me they couldn't watch me slowly kill myself each day, and they gave me an ultimatum. Either I went to treatment or I could no longer live in their house.

Although I had lots of friends, I realized no one's parents would allow me to live with them long term. I was unable to hold down a job to support myself, and I knew I would likely end up on the streets with nowhere to go. I also knew, deep in my heart, that I needed help. But in my warped mind, I was terrified of not being skinny enough to go to an eating disorder treatment center. I was afraid of being treated for an eating disorder and being the fattest girl there! My mom mentioned this to the treatment center staff, and they assured her that it was a common fear and that most of the girls looked normal on the outside. At last, I agreed to go.

I wish this was the turning point for me, the place in my story where I could tell you that the decision completely changed my life and I was healed of my eating disorder forever. But, I was not ready to be well because, in my mind, being "well" meant being fat. And there was no way I was going to allow that to happen.

Despite my fears, I was relieved to find other girls who struggled with the same demons I did, who understood the thoughts and behaviors that seemed so crazy to everyone else. I was given tools for recovery, and my two-month stay in the desert was not at all a waste. I learned that foods like cake and ice cream are not "bad." They just needed to be eaten in moderation. I learned about black-and-white thinking and how to change my "all or nothing" thoughts so that they were more balanced. I also identified my triggers (like looking at magazines of thin, beautiful models) and how to avoid them or handle them. The nutritionist identified the amount of calories and fat I should be ingesting each day for my body to be healthy and taught me how to eat appropriate portions to maintain the weight that was right for me. For the first time, I was given hope that maybe, just maybe, the things I believed about myself were lies and that I didn't have to live like this, that I could actually be free of the eating disorder. And so for a time, I followed the guidelines given by the nutritionist, and I did my best to utilize the tools I'd been given to feed my healthy self instead of the eating disorder.

Just before I went into treatment, I met a guy through my best friend. He wrote me letters regularly and was a tremendous support to me when I came home. Every night, I would cry, and he would hold me, comfort me, and assure me I was going to be okay and that he wouldn't leave me. He seemed to love me and accept me despite my craziness, so, at 21 years old, I married him.

The cavernous holes in my heart yawned wider while I grasped frantically for my husband to fill me. I found my identity in being his wife and being loved by him, even though he isolated me from my friends and family and controlled my comings and goings, belittled me, screamed horrible things at me, and chased me if I tried to get away from him. I didn't recognize that I was being abused, didn't understand that I had become a victim of domestic violence. He began to get drunk regularly and hold parties at our apartment with people who were doing drugs. I grasped for control of my life once again by restricting my food intake and throwing up what little I ate.

When I found evidence my husband was cheating on me, I called my parents to come get me and stayed at their house. He went into a rage when he found out I'd left him, and even though I told him I wanted to work it out and go to counseling, he refused. He told me he wasn't sure he wanted to be married to me anymore.

I remember my world falling out from under me; it felt like a giant had come along and ripped the ground out from under my feet. I was suddenly flailing without an anchor, and I felt my sense of self shattering and splintering inside me. At that moment, I knew for sure I was going to kill myself. I wanted the pain in my heart to end, and I saw no other way. Simultaneously, this other part of me became quite terrified at my hopeless decision and calmly demanded I go tell my parents right that moment what I was thinking. I knew if I didn't tell them immediately the rational part of me would be silenced and it would be too late. My dad held my trembling body, trying to keep me from falling to pieces right there in his arms while my mom called for an ambulance.

I lay in the dark on the hospital bed in the psych ward of a nearby hospital and looked at the bars on the windows. My mom held me in her arms and reminded me that God was still waiting for me with open arms, that He had never left me. In that moment, I realized that God was all I had left. Yes, I had my parents, but I somehow knew they could not fill this gaping hole inside of me and that God was my only hope.

This was a turning point, the beginning of a very long journey down a path of healing into the arms of God, the only One who could complete me and fill the emptiness in my heart. Over the next several days, I felt a strong assurance within my entire body that I did not belong in the psych ward. I watched TV and played cards with other patients who were caught up in addictions, despair, and mental torment that were even worse than what I was experiencing. None of the staff were concerned about whether I ate or didn't, but for some reason I was not focused on losing weight. Something had changed deep inside of me, and I knew that I wanted to be well.

My husband visited me one time in the hospital, and that was the last I ever saw him. He made it clear he no longer wanted to be married to me. He refused to have any contact with me but would not give me a divorce. Finally, my dad helped me find a lawyer, and I filed the papers for divorce. I was 23 years old.

I was engulfed in excruciating pain and fear every waking moment. Sleep was my only reprieve. I would be overcome with adrenaline-filled rage, and my mom would walk with me around the block in the middle of the night, as fast as we could walk to try and get my anger out. She would also walk with me during the day when anxiety gripped my throat like a vise, doing all she could to love me through it. During one of these walks I felt my brain hurtling around in the same circles, ruminating on how hopeless I felt and how I didn't know how to live, didn't know how to fix my situation, or how to make the pain go away.

At that moment, I felt God's firm but gentle voice in my spirit, "Be still and know that I am God." At once, I felt my entire body go still and calm. I was flooded with an unexplainable peace. I had not read the Bible in many years, but I knew this was a verse from my childhood and that God had spoken it to me while supernaturally calming my entire being. I discovered the Psalms and pored over the words of anguish and hope I found there, hungrily grabbing at mouthfuls of scripture throughout the day in moments of fear as if I was starving. And in fact, I was. I had been starving myself of food for years while feeding myself lies. As I swallowed each beautiful, filling verse of Truth, I felt hope glow on my skin once more as His words began to nourish my weakened soul.

Several months after being released from the hospital, I volunteered at a camp for deaf and hard-of-hearing kids. I had always been interested in sign language and had learned the alphabet and a few praise songs as a child in summer camp. During my marriage, even though my husband had been abusive to me and abandoned me, he had at one time encouraged me to learn ASL and had bought me a book on the subject. I was amazed at how I was able to communicate with the children at the camp with the limited number of signs I knew. For the first time in a very long time, I was focused on someone other than myself.

The lady who organized the camp told me about a job opening at one of the public schools for an instructional assistant. She said I was good with children and should look into it. I was given the job as an instructional assistant in an Early Childhood Special Education classroom for children ages two to five with all kinds of disabilities. I looked forward to going to work each day and forgot about the pain in my heart as I poured out my love on these children with special needs. After working there for about a year, I decided to go to school to become an interpreter for the deaf. I attended school at night at the local community college and graduated two and a half years later with a certificate in American Sign Language. I later changed my mind about wanting to be an interpreter and decided I wanted to teach Early Childhood Special Education. This required me to get a graduate degree, and since I had flunked out of college and didn't even have a bachelor's degree, it was going to be a long road. But I was determined. I felt a strong sense of purpose in my life and began to take the necessary classes at the community college to receive an associate's degree.

Meanwhile, I had begun to date an old boyfriend, a guy who had given me my first kiss. He was one of my biggest supporters in helping me go back to school. But he was an atheist, and I knew our relationship could not survive when he felt so strongly about the non-existence of God and I felt so strongly that not only was there a God but that He had rescued me from killing myself and given me hope! And there were other issues. He was abusive, though once again, I didn't recognize it as such. I began listening to my eating disorder again and felt myself secretly spiraling. I was tormented with thoughts of self-harm and would frequently give in to the urges. I also had a war in my head, with two opposing sides screaming at each other throughout the day: *You're fat! You're losing control again by eating! You must lose weight!* and *Don't listen to the lies! You are not fat! You must eat!* Back and forth it went in my head, relentlessly, day after day. I was fractured, split right down the middle; part of me would attempt to eat normally and the other part would roar at me with shame and convince me to throw it all back up again. Then the first part would fold in on itself in shame for having failed again by giving in to my eating disorder. At times, I felt worse than I did before I went to treatment and counseling. At least then it was just the voice of madness from the eating disorder whispering in my ear. This was a fighting match inside my brain, and I didn't even know who I wanted to win.

I stayed with my boyfriend for five years until I finally got the nerve to break up with him after running into another old boyfriend of mine, my first love. We had dated from the time I was 17 to 18 years old, but he had gotten into drugs pretty heavily and cheated on me when I left for college. Now he was a Christian and was clean from drugs and alcohol. It wasn't long before I fell in love with him all over again and we began to date. We got baptized, he for the first time, and me as a rededication of my life to Christ. I began to go with him to NA meetings several times a week to support him in his recovery but quickly discovered that the same principles people used to help them recover from alcohol and drug addiction also applied to recovery from an eating disorder. Soon, I was attending not just to support him, but to gain wisdom and support for myself in my own journey of recovery.

During the meetings, everyone took turns saying, "Hi, my name is____, and I am an addict," as we went around the circle. If you didn't want to talk that night, you would just say, "Pass." I had always introduced myself and then said I was there to support my boyfriend. But one night, I really related to the topic that was being discussed, and I felt an urgency to be real, to be brave and to tell the truth. And so, surrounded by a group of relative strangers, most of them men, I let the words come out, "My name is Krista, and I am in recovery from anorexia and bulimia." And then I began to talk, to release my words into the open, causing the atmosphere to shift and lighten. When I was finished, I felt a sense of fullness and lightness at once, the relief of my body having let go of such a heavy weight. It wasn't a secret anymore. Although my family and friends knew about the eating disorder, as well as my counselors and the other girls at the treatment center, I had never admitted my struggles to anyone else. I felt bravery tingle with newness on my skin as girls came up to me after the meeting and thanked me for opening up and sharing because they, too, were battling an eating disorder, or their daughter was. I met one of my dearest friends because I was brave enough that night to share a piece of my story. We have continued to support each other over the years.

After about a year of dating, my boyfriend and I got married. I was 31 years old, and it had been 10 years since my first marriage. Not long after that, I graduated from college with a bachelor's degree in Sociology and Anthropology and then went on to receive my master's in Early Childhood Special Education. I got a full-time job teaching preschool children with special needs. My husband and I began to read the Bible and pray together and attend church each week. His 11-year-old son came to live with us our second year of marriage, and although it was extremely stressful, I enjoyed being a stepmom and a wife. I was still concerned about gaining weight and was careful about what I ate. I enjoyed eating most of the time but would often unexpectedly feel like I could burst into tears when I was finished. I liked planning and cooking healthy meals for the three of us, and the eating disorder crouched quietly in the back of my head, like a faint buzzing in the background of my life.

Although my husband was clean and in recovery, there were still many demons he was not ready to face, and, not long into our second year of marriage, he quickly began the descent into relapse. One night, when he hadn't come home from drinking at a party, I lay in our bed and thought about the span of my life from the time I was a little girl to all the joys and heartaches in between that had brought me to this moment. Somehow I'd thought I'd left the pain and rubble of my past behind and that everything was going to be fine because I had chosen to follow God now. I had taken a new path where I had married my first love. Now I sat alone on our bed and surveyed the darkness of our bedroom. The outline of the dresser, the open closet door, his green t-shirt balled up on the carpet, the alarm clock on the bedside table that read 2:35 am all appeared to sharpen into focus, and the silence become almost palpable as reality etched its truth onto my heart. I had no idea where my husband was. And there was nothing I could do about it.

All at once, I was assaulted with images from my past. Vivid pictures of myself as a teenager refusing to eat my breakfast and lunch and then secretly throwing up my dinner in the bathroom, slicing my body repeatedly with a razor blade to try to control the pain on the inside, and roaring out my anguish from yet another boyfriend abusing and abandoning me. All these images rushed to the surface in taunting flames of defeat to lick at my skin and threaten to devour me at last. *It will always be like this*, I heard. *You thought you had escaped that life and were making better choices. But you will always screw up because that is who you are.*

As I sat on our bed, anxiety literally shook my body. My teeth chattered together as I realized my life was far out of my control and that I should have paid attention to the red flags before getting married again. The pain was so intense I felt I was burning alive. For a brief moment I felt every nerve within me tense in preparation to run from the pain, to seize whatever means necessary to escape. Then, just as quickly, I realized all the coping methods I had used in the past would worsen the situation. None of it would save me. It would not save my husband, and it would not save my marriage. There was nothing. Nothing I could do but surrender, to lay it all down in its ugliness, bare and exposed, a chaotic heap of trash, and release it from my grasp at Jesus' feet. Just relinquish it and feel the pain, stop running from it. There is a verse in the Bible that says, "He feeds on ashes, a deluded heart misleads him; he cannot save himself or say, 'Is not this thing in my right hand a lie?'" (Isaiah 44:20). All this time, I'd believed that recovery meant giving up the fight to be in control and surrendering instead to being out of control and fat. I thought the eating disorder would keep me safe, but I had been feeding on ashes, a dusty, charred pile of lies.

And so I lay down in the fire. Every fiber of my being screamed with pain and begged for me to resist, but I knew the situation was only getting worse and was so far out of my control there was no use even trying to manage it. So instead of flailing my body around and struggling to escape, I just let the flames devour me, let the pain burn its way from deep inside my soul out onto the surface of my skin. As I faced it at last, I thought about all the many ways I had tried to run from pain in general, pain that relentlessly chased me with the ultimate intent to destroy me. It seemed to all culminate in this moment, and, strangely enough, I felt the best solution was to relax into it and cease my fighting.

And just like years before, when I was wracked with anger and anxiety, speed walking around the block with Mom in the middle of the night, I heard, "Be still my child, Krista, and know that I am God."

In that moment, I surrendered it all to Him, the abuse and mistakes of my past, my marriage and my husband, the eating disorder and self-harm, depression and anxiety, and perhaps most importantly, my will. I let go of my perceived control over my life and finally believed that the methods of controlling my food intake or harming my body were not tools of safety but of imprisonment. I finally believed that surrendering to a loving, trustworthy God who made my body and had good plans for my life, who did not intend to harm me but to give me hope and a future, was not an indication of failure but a gateway to freedom.

In the days that followed, I would whisper over and over, "I trust you, God, I trust you, God," and for the first time in years, I clung to Him with all my might and let go of the eating disorder and its rotten lies.

And then one night my husband confused the closet for the toilet because he was so drunk, and when I tried to help him, he swung at my face. I ducked, and he missed. The next day, when I told him he had tried to hit me, he shrugged his shoulders and said he didn't remember doing that and was sorry. But he wasn't sorry enough to stop drinking or get help.

At first, he went to counseling with me and even started to go back to NA meetings. But the pain was too deep for him to face, and, in the end, he chose drinking over me. Once again, my world crumbled as I received the divorce papers and accepted the fact that another husband had abandoned me. The pain from this second divorce, coupled with pain from the first, was unimaginable. But this time, something had changed in me, and it was different.

I immersed myself in prayer and scripture, and with the help of a counselor, my family, and friends, gradually crawled out of the toxic wreckage that had become my life and into new possibilities and hope. I took a ballet class, something I had started and stopped several times over the course of my life because I could never stop obsessing over my weight and comparing my body with the other girls'. This time, I took the class with my tummy swollen with gas from the IBS that plagued me, and I did not compare myself to others. Instead, I felt my heart sprout wings and soar around inside me with happiness as I performed with the other women on stage in front of an audience. I began to bravely try new things like paddleboarding and surf yoga. And I fell head over heels in love with kickboxing. I started to enjoy eating food, to exercise with the goal of being strong and healthy as opposed to being thin, to grocery shop without having a panic attack, and to try out new recipes. I bought a condo and began to create mixed media art as another means of self expression, in addition to my writing.

I still struggle with my body image at times and have to be careful not to cross that thin line that stands as a barrier between exercising to be healthy and exercising to be thin. I am still learning to eat when I'm hungry and stop when I'm full. I stay away from images and messages that encourage dieting and being thin, study the Bible and pray daily, memorize scripture, post positive messages all around my house, and keep a gratitude journal. When I feel myself starting to waver, to give in to those old lies that tell me being thin will make me lovable and keep me safe and in control, I remind myself how far I've come and tell myself the truth:

I am fearfully and wonderfully made. (Psalm 139:14)

I am God's work of art. (Ephesians 2:10)

God has a good purpose for my life. (Jeremiah 29:11)

I am chosen and dearly loved by God. (Colossians 3:12)

The eating disorder lies to me! It cannot save me! (Isaiah 44:20)

Being thin cannot keep me safe. Only God can keep me safe. He is my hope, my security and and my salvation (Proverbs 29:25, Isaiah 30:12-14 and Psalm 62:5-6)

Nothing can separate me from His love. (Romans 8:39)

The truth always gets me back on track again. It just took me a long time to believe the truth over the lies.

I don't want you to think that my life is wrapped up all neatly in a bow now and that's the end of my story. I still battle depression and anxiety, have been diagnosed with Complex PTSD, and see a counselor to help me persevere in facing my pain and finding healing. But I have found tools to better manage these issues. I am a survivor of verbal, emotional, and sexual abuse, and the eating disorder no longer dominates my life! Do you know what a miracle that is for me to even say those words?

No key moment has been the turning point for my recovery. It has been a process, a journey, and my story is not yet finished. I am just far enough along the path now to call back to you who may be living in the shadows, stumbling crippled through the tunnel, believing there's no way out. I am here to tell you, there is! It is not an easy path, but it is worth it. And you are not alone!

The first step of reaching out for help is perhaps the hardest. The eating disorder will scream at you that it knows best and that getting well and eating food in a healthy way will only make you fat and weak and out of control. I know I cannot make you believe me when I tell you these are lies. I just want you to know that you can be free and you don't have to feed on ashes anymore. You are worth recovery. You can do this. Reach out for help and take the first step. Then take another. Don't you dare give up. There is hope, and you can learn to love your body, let go, and enjoy your life. I am praying for you, shouting for you up ahead in the distance to JUST KEEP GOING.

I promise you it will be worth it.

I am living proof.

Krista is a Special Education teacher who enjoys reading, writing, creating mixed media art, listening to music, practicing yoga, paddleboarding, kickboxing, and being with family and friends in her free time. She loves writing poetry and is currently working on a spiritual memoir about her healing journey. She is passionate about using her words and art to give encouragement to other women who are suffering and helping them to know God and find freedom.

If you could see me, you would see me fighting every day to hear that voice—the voice of courage and grace and grit that brings me out of those dark places and back to life day after day after day.

—Christina Tinker

If You Could See Me

Christina Tinker

Hi, my name is Christina and I'm a recovering anorexic perfectionist. I'm a wife and a mother of the most incredible children. My ten-year-old, Alexander, is as smart as a whip and has the compassion of Ghandi most days. My six-year-old twins, Andrew and Anastasia, are funny and kind beyond their years.

How is it possible that they are so incredible—damn near perfect—coming from the likes of me?

I guess you can see why I consider myself to be recovering. It's this type of thinking that plagues the inner dialogue of a serial perfectionist who is riddled with anxiety most days.

Most people who know me consider me to be outgoing and often the life of the party. My husband says I can light up any room with my smile. He thinks very highly of me—too highly most days. He thinks I'm capable of anything and calls me brave and courageous.

You'd likely never guess it looking at my smiling face, but if you could see me, you would see that some days I am scared and small and trapped inside my own head.

Some days I still wake thinking of what I should and shouldn't eat that day. A dread comes over me as I think of what pants will or won't fit and if I should try to squeeze in an early morning workout not for the joy of it, but to burn a few more calories in the hopes that my thighs might not touch that day.

I still sometimes walk into my bathroom to take a shower and when I emerge clean and fresh, smelling like sweet lavender, I turn my back to the mirror as I wrap the towel around my shoulders, avoiding at all costs the reflection of my naked body.

On bad days, after I dry off and slather my soft, smooth skin with lotion, careful to keep my back turned from the mirror, I walk into my closet and put on the *skinny control pants* I never actually wear out. I have to make sure the button will snap before I can move forward with my day. On the worst days, that single moment of the button snapping or not snapping could decide the fate of my day. If the button snapped and the zipper could be zipped, I could go on about my business knowing I had kept things *under control* another day. If it didn't snap...I had a very different kind of day.

More than a decade after claiming recovery from anorexia and bulimia, there are still days when I hate this body of mine that just won't shrink to the size of my satisfaction. It's as if there's a tape recorder on repeat saying things like, *You'll never be good enough. Who do you think you are? Or what if something happens to one of the kids? What if you lose him? What if there's no more money? What if you never become the woman you were born to be?*

If you could see me, you would know that none of this has anything to do with my actual body or the actual size of my hips or my thighs or anything else. It has to do with my need for control and the fear that I could actually lose something I care so much about.

When I was 16 years old, I had a pretty perfect life, and I'm not looking through rose-colored glasses when I say that. Our family was like a modern-day version of the Waltons. My parents were and still are pillars of their community. My brother, sister, and I were darling, diligent students *(if I do say so myself)*. Even at 16, I had not found the typical rebellious teenage life to be alluring. We were and are a close-knit family. On the Sunday after Spring Break 1994, my younger brother was invited to go with some friends to a farm about 30 minutes away. One of the friends had just started driving.

I don't remember how long he was gone before our phone rang. This was the late '90s, and my parents had just built a beautiful house that had one of those fancy media rooms. The four of us—my mom, dad, and younger sister and I—were in there watching TV when that phone call came in. I clearly recall the world changing in that moment. My normally expressive mother was almost robotic in her response: "Where? When? How?" Then she hung up, looked at me and said, "There's been an accident. We have to go to the hospital. Watch your sister and I'll call you when we can."

I don't remember speaking to her again for at least 24 hours. I think I took my sister to school the next morning. Then an uncle or a grandparent showed up and told us we needed to go to the hospital. My parents would not be coming home anytime soon.

My only brother, just weeks before turning 14 years old, was brain-dead in a coma. He remained there for weeks, machines keeping him alive. I remember going into the room and reading letters our friends had sent to him. I remember the buzz of the machines breathing for him and the sad, hollow faces of my mother and father.

No one from the hospital staff ever really said anything to me or my sister, who was not yet 10 at the time. Looking back as an adult involved in children's mental health advocacy work, I think they were waiting for him to die.

Then, they would have offered us grief counseling. They would have introduced us to child psychologists and suggested a support group for siblings. But he didn't die. In fact, over the course of many long, hard months he had an almost complete and miraculous recovery. He learned to walk and talk again. Today he is a husband and has two beautiful daughters.

But trauma doesn't go away when the miracle comes.

If you could see me, you would know that sometimes I'm so scared of the beauty and the depth of this life I've been given I can hardly breathe. You would see that my need for control is as real to me as my need for air and water.

If you could see me, you would see that even in the midst of all this fear and anxiety, I'm able to find that small, still voice deep inside my soul that quiets all the madness.

To me, the gift of my anxiety is the heightened sense of awareness and empathy it brings to my life.

You see, if I turned off those voices that told me not to look into the mirror when I'm naked or threatened something terrible might happen to one of my beloved children, I would be turning off the voice that allows me to see the very face of God when I look at my daughter.

I would be turning off the voice that says even though I am flawed and far from perfect, this kind, generous man loves me faithfully and fiercely and chooses to walk through life by my side.

If you could see me, you would see me fighting every day to hear that voice—the voice of courage and grace and grit that brings me out of those dark places and back to life day after day after day.

Christina Tinker is a corporate storyteller and courage cultivator™. She is passionate about sharing stories that transform our lives personally and professionally. This story was originally developed through Christina's work with the project #IfYouCouldSeeMe. Christina's passion to inspire people and bring them together in a way that is authentic and brave drives her to create a community that will change the world for the better one story at a time.

Resources

National Eating Disorders Association, nationaleatingdisorders.org

Beating Eating Disorders, beatingeatingdisorders.com

Eating Disorder Hope, eatingdisorderhope.com

Beat Eating Disorders, beateatingdisorders.org

Mirror Mirror Eating Disorder Help, mirror-mirror.org

National Association of Anorexia Nervosa and Associated Disorders, anad.org

Center for Discovery, centerfordiscovery.com

Author Links and Contacts

Alison Beining:

00karma90@gmail.com

Catherine Brown:

www.facebook.com/writercatherinebrown

www.linkedin.com/in/catherine-brown-writer/

www.catherinebrownwriter.com

Christina Tinker:

https://www.christinatinkertalks.com

https://www.linkedin.com/in/christinatinkertalks/

Francis Iacobucci:

www.instagram.com/francisiacobucci

www.linkedin.com/in/francisiacobucci/

francisiacobucci@gmail.com

Krista Hutcherson:

www.instagram.com/kristajoy.wildflower

Mark:

markspersonalexodus@gmail.com

MJ Mars:

www.twitter.com/chelle8854

www.instagram.com/mjmarsauthor

Nina Ward:

https://www.facebook.com/ninawardwrites

https://www.linkedin.com/in/ninaward/

Rebecca Evans:

https://revans33.wordpress.com/

www.instagram.com/rebeccawrites33

www.facebook.com/rebeccaevanswrites

www.twitter.com/RebeccaWrites

Terri Porter:

terriporter1@gmail.com

Sarah:

www.happyjoyousaf

www.twitter.com/happyjoyousAF

www.instagram.com/happyjoyousAF

www.facebook.com/happyjoyousAF

CPSIA information can be obtained
at www.ICGtesting.com
Printed in the USA
LVHW031002140721
692650LV00002B/177